Tours of Cape Cod

Andrew G. Buckley

Schiffer Publishing Ltd

4880 Lower Valley Road, Atglen, PA 19310

Schiffer Books are available at special discounts for bulk purchases for sales promotions or premiums. Special editions, including personalized covers, corporate imprints, and excerpts can be created in large quantities for special needs. For more information contact the publisher:

Published by Schiffer Publishing Ltd.
4880 Lower Valley Road
Atglen, PA 19310
Phone: (610) 593-1777; Fax: (610) 593-2002
E-mail: Info@schifferbooks.com

For the largest selection of fine reference books on this and related subjects,
please visit our web site at **www.schifferbooks.com**
We are always looking for people to write books on new and related subjects.
If you have an idea for a book please contact us at the above address.

This book may be purchased from the publisher.
Include $3.95 for shipping.
Please try your bookstore first.
You may write for a free catalog.

In Europe, Schiffer books are distributed by
Bushwood Books
6 Marksbury Ave.
Kew Gardens
Surrey TW9 4JF England
Phone: 44 (0) 20 8392-8585; Fax: 44 (0) 20 8392-9876
E-mail: info@bushwoodbooks.co.uk
Website: www.bushwoodbooks.co.uk
Free postage in the U.K., Europe; air mail at cost.

Copyright © 2008 by Andrew G. Buckley
Library of Congress Control Number: 2008921041

Designed by rOs
Type set in Shelly Andante BT heading font/text font Zurich BT

ISBN: 978-0-7643-3023-0
Printed in China

Contents

Sand in my Shoes

Living on Cape Cod means that every person you have ever met in your entire life will come visit you. I heard this once when I was a kid, the youngest of five in a family that had roots going back almost 400 years. "Camp Buckley," as the homestead on the Oyster Pond in Chatham became known, hosted every person I had ever known — times six (to include my mother). You didn't make it out of adolescence without becoming an accomplished tour guide for the place.

Cape Codders, from way back, were great travelers. Plenty of sea captains and crews of merchantman and whalers would ship out from these shores for multi-year voyages to the far ends of the earth for one simple reason: economic desperation.

Up until a few decades ago, most of the Cape was very poor. The soil was often sterile or sandy. We were too far from the centers of capital and migration. And the waters were so treacherous that ships would give the Cape a wide berth. If we wanted to learn or to earn, we knew we'd have to go fairly far away. Still, the beauty of the place kept a hold on us. More than once I've been told to sprinkle a little sand in my shoes before an extended period away from the Cape, to insure a safe return.

As a traveler, I've avoided tours and relied either on friends from the area or serendipity to find my way about, observing the axiom of Cape Cod transplant Paul Theroux: "Tourists don't know where they've been, travelers don't know where they're going."

This is not a traditional walking tour book. I have avoided giving a presentation that is simply a recapitulation of what one might hear from a docent or read on a plaque. Instead, I have put this together with plenty of images to entice you to go off on your own. But I have written it as if I were sitting in the passenger seat, giving the directions and a offering occasional commentary. Every place might not be your cup of tea — they might not be mine, either. But let's check it out and see what happens.

How to Use this Book

Rule #1: No one ever said you had to walk a walking tour. Of the six tours in this book, two are in densely built downtowns, where parking (free or otherwise) is at a premium. Chatham, is best suited for a casual bike ride. You could walk the Canal tour — if you're truly hardcore — but it is best suited for a mix of biking, driving, and walking. The Outer Cape and Route 6A tours are really meant to be driven.

Rule #2: No one ever said you had to do a whole tour at once. Once you actually get into P-Town or Woods Hole, you'll probably want to do these shorter tours in their entirety. But the Route 6A tour could take the better part of a day.

Rule #3: No one ever claimed these tours were comprehensive. I've left out plenty. The towns of Mashpee, Harwich, Brewster, and Truro — all with rich and varied histories, don't even make an appearance. I omit them simply because they did not lend themselves to be part of any of the other tours. I had intended on extending the Route 6A tour through Brewster (home to my grandmother, Adeline Eldridge), but it proved to be one town too many. The same applies to Truro with the Outer Cape. Harwich couldn't be added to Chatham unless we were going to throw out the idea that it was walkable. Mashpee is really off the beaten path — which shows why it was chosen as a Indian reservation back in the nineteenth century.

As for Hyannis, the local chambers of commerce have been hawking that area since John Kennedy was nominated for president. As stated previously, this book is written as if I were in the passenger seat of your car, showing you where to go. Or, in the case of Hyannis, where not to.

Rule #4: Not everything is open. Well, sometimes we're too early in the day. Or they're only open on Tuesdays. Or only in the summer. Rather than recite hours and days open — which can change year-to-year — I've included contact info. And if you can't get into every single place, no big deal. Most of these places have been around a century of more. They're not going anywhere.

The Cape Cod Canal entrance from Buzzards Bay. *Courtesy of US Army Corps of Engineers.*

Cape Cod Canal Railroad Bridge. *Courtesy of US Army Corps of Enginee*

Drive and Walk or Bike Tour 1

In the Beginning...

The Canal and Sandwich

Before the Cape Cod Canal was finished in 1916, Cape Cod was Barnstable County, meaning the 13 towns of Provincetown, Truro, Wellfleet, Eastham, Orleans, Chatham, Harwich, Brewster, Dennis, Yarmouth, Barnstable, Mashpee, Falmouth, Sandwich, and Bourne. Once the shortcut for shipping was made, there were small slices of Sandwich and Bourne left hanging on the mainland. No one on this side of the Bourne and Sagamore Bridges considers these orphaned areas as Cape Cod... but we're still starting off there.

The Cape Cod Railroad Bridge is adjacent to our first stop. After the Army Corps of Engineers took over the Canal, the Works Progress Administration built the vertical lift bridge in the 1930s to carry rail traffic on and off the Cape. It is primarily used for the "trash train," carrying our refuse to a waste-to-energy plant off-Cape, and for the Cape Cod Railroad's scenic train in season.

Overall Distance: 13.4 miles
Time: 4 hours
Public Restrooms: Canal Area Chamber of Commerce, Canal Visitors Center, Sandwich center

Note: Two things to consider about the end of this trip when starting off. The Cape Cod Central Railroad runs scenic trains in the afternoons from Sandwich Depot to Hyannis — call the railroad for times. If you'd rather end at the Sandwich Boardwalk and Town Neck Beach, try to get there *after* 4 PM in the summer, or you'll pay a hefty parking fee.

Drive or walk/bike? Most people will want to drive the first leg, from Buzzards Bay and Bourne to Sandwich, and walk most of the rest. But the Cape Cod Canal is lined flanked by flat access roads which double as bike paths. So if you're up for the 6.5 mile leg in between, this tour has the most to offer for those on two wheels, with little variation.

National Marine Life Center. *Author's photo.*

Juvenile pilot whale skeleton. National Marine Life Center. *Author's photo.*

1) National Marine Life Center
120 Main Street, Buzzard's Bay, MA
508 743-9888
www.nmlc.org

Directions:
The National Marine Life Center is located just a few doors down Main Street from the Canal Area Chamber of Commerce in Buzzards Bay. This is on the mainland side of the Cape Cod Canal, near the Bourne Bridge.

Find your way to the Buzzards Bay Rotary, which is the intersection of Routes 28 and 6, and look for the sign for the Mass Maritime Academy. Continue on Main Street, keeping Pier Road, the Academy entrance, and the Railroad Depot on your right. Look on your right for the NMLC sign and turn into the parking lot with the whales on the building.

Description:
This low, unassuming building with the big murals is a hospital for stranded marine animals. The Cape's elongated hook shape and the close proximity to the warm waters of the Gulf Stream means a high casualty rate for whales, turtles, and the like. NMLC is a great place to start off a tour of the Cape, whose residents historically depended upon these animals for their much of their livelihood. If you're including a whale watch, seal tour, or visit to an aquarium while in the area, a stop into the here is a fun way to become the resident expert. Open seasonally.

National Marine Life Center. *Author's photo.*

Joseph Jefferson Windmill.
Author's photo.

Aptucxet Trading Post entrance.
Author's photo.

2) Aptuxcet Trading Post
24 Aptucxet Rd., Bourne, MA
508 759-9487
www.bournehistoricalsoc.org
• Distance: 3.3 miles
• Driving Time: 10 minutes

Directions:
Leaving the parking lot, turn right and continue on Main Street for 0.9 miles. You will enter the a rotary (although it is more square than round). Stay to the left at first and watch for the signs to the Bourne Bridge and Falmouth. Switch to the right lane, and once on the ramp, bear right again. When you are heading onto the Bourne Bridge, stay in the right lane.

As the bridge empties into the Bourne Rotary, take your first exit onto Trowbridge Road. Continue for 0.6 miles, through the intersection with County and Sandwich Roads. Trowbridge becomes Shore Road now. After 0.3 miles, turn right onto Old Monument Neck Road. Go under the railroad, then take an immediate right onto Aptuxcet Road.

Take Aptuxcet Road 300 feet and look for the windmill on your left. Enter the driveway immediately after and park on the right.

Description:
The first thing you should know about Bourne is that it used to be the western half of Sandwich—the poor boonies as compared to the rich village with the glass factory. The second thing is that it hosted the summer White House of President Grover Cleveland. The windmill was the art studio of Joseph Jefferson, boon companion of the Cleveland. The two would often hunt piping plovers in the summer — a violation of the Endangered Species Act that would have put the former Chief Magistrate in the hole at $25,000 per beak.

Gray Gables Depot. *Author's photo.*

President Grover Cleveland in 1888.
Courtesy of the Library of Congress.

Aptucxet Trading Post. *Author's photo.*

Before the Canal, this narrowest part of the isthmus has been used as for portage by traders between Buzzards Bay and Cape Cod Bay. In 1627, the Pilgrims from the Plymouth Colony started a post here to take advantage of the strategic position for trade with the local Wampanoag and the Dutch in New York. The current house is a replica built in 1930.

Adjacent to the trading post is the Gray Gables Depot built for President Cleveland's personal use. It was moved to this site in 1976. If you continue further along the path, you'll see the Canal, the bike path, and the Railroad bridge to your left.

Briggs-McDermott House. *Author's photo.*

Alonzo Booth
Blacksmith Shop.
Author's photo.

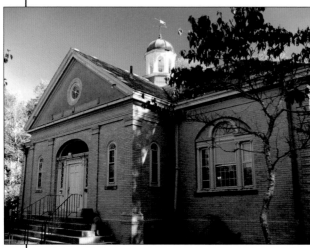

Jonathan Bourne
Historic Center.
Author's photo.

3) Briggs-McDermott House

20 Sandwich Road, Bourne, MA 02532
508 759-8167
www.bournehistoricalsoc.org
• Distance: 0.5 miles
• Driving Time: 2 minutes

Directions:

Turn left onto Aptuxcet Road and follow for 0.2 miles to the stop sign. Turn right onto Perry Ave and drive over the railroad bridge to Sandwich Road. Take a left on Sandwich Road and drive 0.1 miles. Look for the tall yellow colonial on the right. You can either pull into the small parking space just before it, or across the street at the library.

George Briggs, another friend of President Cleveland's, was a town father of Bourne and active in local politics. His house has been restored to reflect the time he resided there in the later half of the nineteenth century.

Description:

The Alonzo Booth Blacksmith Shop, built in 1888, was moved to these grounds and restored in 1998. The story goes that President Cleveland's horses were shod here and it remains a working forge. If you want to watch, call the Bourne Historical for times.

4) Jonathan Bourne Historical Center

30 Keene Street, Bourne, MA
508 759-8167
• Distance: 0.2 miles
• Driving Time: 1 minute

Directions:

From the McDermott House, turn right onto Sandwich Road, go for almost 200 feet, then take the next left onto Keene Street. The road goes straight, then turns right. The driveway for the center will be on your right.

Description:

Jonathan Bourne, who made his fortune in whaling, was the state legislator who worked to help Bourne separate from Sandwich, and was thus honored by having the new town named after him in 1884. This building was given to the town as a library by his daughter in 1897, in his memory. If there are budding archaeologists with you, challenge them to decipher the ancient markings on the Bourne Stone. Open year-round on limited hours.

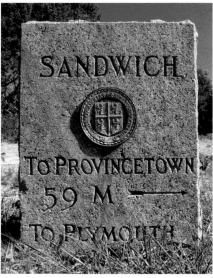

Old King's Highway marker: Bourne-Sandwich line. *Author's photo.*

Old King's Highway marker: Sandwich-Bourne line. *Author's photo.*

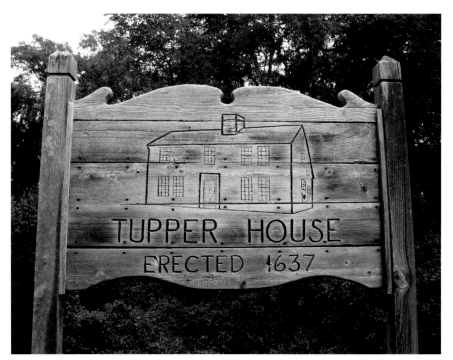

Tupper House, Sandwich. *Author's photo.*

5) Tupper House Monument
19 Tupper Road, Sandwich, MA
- Distance: 5.4 miles
- Driving Time: 13 minutes

Directions:
Turn right out of the driveway, onto Keene Street. Keene curves right and back to Sandwich Road. At the stop sign, turn left.

Continue on Sandwich Road under the Bourne Bridge, for 0.6 miles. At the stop sign with Route 6A, bear left to continue along Sandwich Road, keeping the canal on your left and passing under the Sagamore Bridge.

After 4.2 miles, you will see the state road sign "Entering Sandwich" on your right. You may also notice the small stone markers for Sandwich and Bourne, unique to Route 6A on the Cape.

After another 0.1 mile, look for the sign for Sandwich Marina and turn left onto Tupper Road.

Follow Tupper for 0.3 miles and look for the wooden sign for the Tupper House on your right. A small parking area is adjacent.

(NOTE TO BIKERS: When Keene road turns right, you should turn left, heading toward the Canal, and take a right onto the trail. By taking this Route, you will be bypassing Tupper House. Follow trail signs to the Canal Visitor's Center, approximately 6 miles away).

> *The oldest Sandwich house still extant is the Tupper house, in which that race have dwelt since the settlement of the town, and which has features in rustic New England architecture worthy the attention of the curious. In its large kitchen a tall man can hardly stand up right, and the house has a super-garret.*
> -- Rev. N.H. Chamberlain, *New England Magazine*, 1889

Description:
The Nye family genealogy recalls that Katherine Tupper married Benjamin Nye here "in the new Tupper homestead" on October 19, 1640. Just a marker remains now. Look nearby for the entrance to the old orchard.

Canal Visitors Center. *Author's photo.*

The Cape Cod Canal entrance from Cape Cod Bay. *Courtesy of US Army Corps of Engineers.*

The schooner *Roseway* sails past the Canal Visitors Center. *Author's photo.*

Rangers conduct interpretive programs at Canal Visitors Center. *Courtesy of US Army Corps of Engineers.*

6) Canal Visitors Center

60 Ed Moffitt Drive, Sandwich, MA
508 833-9678
www.nae.usace.army.mil/recreati/ccc/
    recreation/recreation.htm
• Distance: 1.1 miles
• Driving Time: 3 minutes

Directions:

Take a right back onto Tupper Road and continue for another half mile. Look for the Cape Cod Canal sign and turn left onto Freezer Road. After 0.1 miles, as you see the Sandwich Marina, take a right onto Ed Moffitt Drive. Follow Ed Moffitt Drive for 0.4 mile, keeping the marina on your left. Watch for the Coast Guard Station on your right, and turn right to continue on Ed Moffitt Drive. Keeping the Canal on your left, follow Ed Moffit to the end. The Visitors Center is well-marked.

"Kieth Car Company and Bridge, Sagamore, Mass." Canal Construction during Belmont's era, circa 1913. *Courtesy of US Army Corps of Engineers.*

Description:

Aside from anglers, the Visitors Center is a well-kept secret. Situated at the eastern end of the Canal, it provides a perfect spot to watch ship traffic passing to and from Cape Cod Bay. Inside the center, the Army Corps has everything you ever wanted to know about the Cape Cod Canal but forgot to ask. They also host programs, walks, and informational movies. If you have the chance, walk down the bike path to the stone jetty or relax in the rocking chairs on the veranda. You never can tell what might cruise by.

Sandwich
Glass
Museum.
*Author's
photo.*

Contemporary
work of the
Sandwich
Glass
Museum.
*Author's
photo.*

Glass blowing demonstration at the Sandwich
Glass Museum. *Author's photo.*

7) Sandwich Glass Museum

129 Main Street, Sandwich, MA
508 888-0251
www.sandwichglassmuseum.org
• Distance: 1.2 miles
• Driving Time: 4 minutes

Directions:

From the parking lot, follow Ed Moffit Drive and take your first left onto Coast Guard Road. Follow Coast Guard Road to a stop sign, then bear right onto Town Neck Road. Continue on Town Neck Road for 0.3 miles, cross the railroad tracks and take a left onto Tupper Road. After another 0.2 miles, there will be a stop light at the intersection with Route 6A. Go straight and continue on Tupper Road for another 0.4 miles. Look on the left for the Glass Museum's parking lot and pull in.

Description:

The Sandwich Glass Museum, while focused on the industry that made the town rich in the 1800s, also promotes the history of the Cape's oldest town as a whole. While there, you can watch a live glass blowing demonstration or sign up for one of their own guided walking tours (if you haven't had enough already!).

8) Dexter Grist Mill & Newcomb Tavern

2 Water Street, Sandwich, MA
508 888-4910
• Distance: 500 feet
• Walking Time: 1 minute

Directions:

Exiting the museum, take a left on Tupper Road. At the intersection with Main Street you will see the Civil War monument, with a soldier standing atop a high pillar. To your right will be a small traffic island with a stone marker dedicated to Benjamin Nye and Katherine Tupper, the newlyweds previously mentioned.

Turn left and continue along the sidewalk to the crosswalk just after the Town Hall. As you cross, you will see the small drinking fountain. Turn left onto the sidewalk and walk another 100 feet up Water Street to the entrance to the mill, to the rear of Town Hall.

Dexter's Grist Mill. *Author's photo.*

Description:

The mill was built here at the foot of Shawme Pond in the 1640s, not too many years after the founding of the town. It was restored in 1961, and in season it still grinds and sells corn meal. Ask a about a combination ticket to the mill and Hoxie House, just up the street.

Newcomb Tavern. *Author's photo.*

It is embellished with a large and beautiful pond of water in its centre, and a fall of water, on which are situated a gristmill and fulling-mill that are supplied from an inexhaustible fountain. This stream shapes its course to the sea, fertilizing the lands and meadows through which it passes. Round this pond stand the principal houses of the village, together with a number of shops for the different mechanick arts. The meeting house of the first precinct and a handsome academy occupy two neighbouring eminences. There are two publick inns in this village, which are excelled by few, if any, in the State.

— Wendell Davis, Description of Sandwich, in the County of Barnstable Massachusetts, 1802.

Description:

A latecomer compared to the Tupper House and grist mill, the Newcomb Tavern was only built in 1693. During the Revolutionary War, it was a gathering spot for Loyalists — in opposition to the better known Dan'l Webster Inn, just block away, which was the local headquarters for Patriots. Newcomb Tavern is now rented out as a vacation home.

Thornton W. Burgess Museum. *Author's photo.*

Hoxie House, from Shawme Pond. *Author's photo.*

Hoxie House, from Water Street. *Author's photo.*

9) Thornton W. Burgess Museum
4 Water Street (Route 130), Sandwich, MA
508-888-4668/6870
www.thorntonburgess.org
• Distance: 500 feet
• Walking Time: 2 minutes

Directions:
Leaving the mill as you came in, turn right on the sidewalk and continue up Water Street, keeping Shawme Pond on your right. The Burgess Museum will be the first house on your right.

Description:
The home of native son Thornton Burgess, prolific nature and children's writer, now features exhibits on his life and works. It also houses the Sandwich Chamber of Commerce. In season, children's bedtime stories are hosted here.

10) Hoxie House
18 Water Street, Sandwich
508-888-1173
• Distance: 750 feet
• Walking Time: 3 minutes

Directions:
Cross Water Street to the sidewalk and take a right. Continue up Water Street with the pond on your right for 650 feet. Look for the Hoxie House sign on your right, and cross Water Street again.

Description:
The oldest house in the oldest town on Cape Cod, Hoxie House was built in 1675. It has been restored to reflect the period. From the hill overlooking Shawme Pond, it is easy to see why, when they had the whole of the town to settle upon, they chose this spot.

Sandwich Depot. *Author's photo.*

Cape Cod Rail Road across Hoxie Pond in Sandwich. Courtesy of CCRR

Boston & Sandwich
Glass Works marker.
Author's photo.

11) Sandwich Depot
Jarves Street, Sandwich, MA 02563
888 797-RAIL
www.capetrain.com
- Distance: 1660 feet (walking) plus 0.5 miles driving
- Time: 9 minutes

Directions:
From the Hoxie House driveway, cross Water Street again, take a left on the sidewalk and return to your car. From the Glass Museum, turn left onto Tupper Road, then another onto Main Street. Just after Town Hall, bear left at the fork to continue on Main Street and keep the tall white spire of the Congregational Church on your right.

Continue for another 0.2 miles on Main Street, passing the Dan'l Webster Inn on your left. Turn left onto Jarves Street. At the stop lights with Route 6A, continue straight on Jarves for another 0.1 mile. The depot parking lot is on the right.

Description:
Rather than running through the center of town, the railroad was laid out to run adjacent to the center of industry — the glass factory. If you're not interested in catching the random passing of the trash train from Yarmouth, wait for the scenic train between Hyannis and the canal to stop in the afternoons from May to October.

12) Boston & Sandwich Glass Factory Monument
Jarves Street & Factory Streets,
Sandwich, MA
- Distance: 500 feet
- Driving Time: 1 minute

Directions:
From the depot parking lot, turn right onto Jarves, cross the tracks and continue for one more block. At the intersection of Factory, look for the squat, flat marker across the street to the left.

Sandwich Boardwalk. *Author's pho*

Sandwich Boardwalk. *Author's pho*

Description:
The glass factory was here. Look at the relief map of the area. It was huge. Now look at the area. A collection of smaller houses on a marsh. Hard to believe that a going concern that made $30 million in the space of 60 years in the mid-1800s has been swept from the earth so completely. Railroad expansion to the West, with cheaper competitors, ended the glass factory in Sandwich. As I heard tell, they were always at a disadvantage, though. On the peninsula of Cape Cod, the iron content in the sand was too high, so the factory had to import its chief raw material. Call up your high school English teacher and ask if they can think of a better example of true "irony."

12) Sandwich Boardwalk
Boardwalk Road, Sandwich, MA
508-888-5884
• Distance: 500 feet
• Driving Time: 1 minute

Directions:
With your back to the marker, facing Factory Road, take a right. Continue on Factory Road for one block and take a right onto Harbor Road. As the road bears to the left, it becomes Boardwalk Road. Follow this to the parking lot at the end.

Description:
At over 1,000 feet long, the boardwalk leads across Mill Creek to Town Neck Beach. A previous boardwalk was destroyed by Hurricane Bob in 1991, and this was rebuilt through volunteer contributions — look for names of benefactors among the 1700 planks.

This is as good a place to stop as any, unless you want to jump on the scenic train. I have made a glaring omission here — Heritage Museums & Gardens just outside of Sandwich Village. It sits on 100 acre and contains numerous displays and exhibits. I encourage you to visit and make the most of the price of admission by spending the better part of a day there.

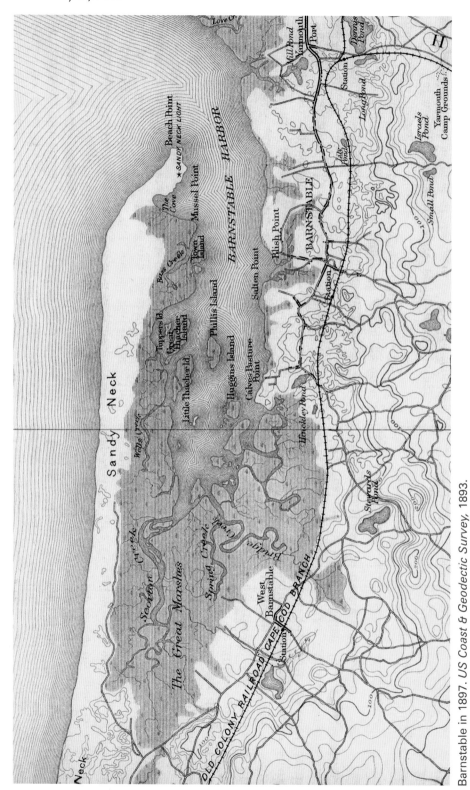

Barnstable in 1897. *US Coast & Geodectic Survey*, 1893.

Drive and Walk Tour 2:

Antiques, Old Books, Stone Walls, and Cranberries.

Route 6A through Barnstable,

Cummaquid, Yarmouth Port,

and Dennis

Overall Distance: 16.6 miles
Time: 5 hours
Public Restrooms: Sturgis Library, Barnstable Superior Courthouse, Coast Guard Heritage Museum, Cape Cod Museum of Art, Sesuit Harbor (seasonally)

Note: This is a long one, and you could easily break it in two… or skip a few things. No offense will be taken by this writer. Depending upon the time of day, you could take an extended lunch along with all the attorneys in Barnstable village, or set up camp at Parnassus Books in Yarmouth Port. But try to get to the end the trail by sunset… because this route, like a classic novel, has a happy ending.

Also, take care if you're going to bike this. While there are plenty of narrow, windy roads just made for bikes, there are plenty of drivers who aren't aware of this. Frequently there is no shoulder to the road at all. Speed is not the problem with the traffic — it is that, rather than pull over, looky loos from far and wide will pay more attention to pointing out scenery than they will to the course their car is taking.

Drivers: please be aware. You are sharing a road that was set down well before horses even arrived on these shores. The residents like to keep it narrow. Being the biggest thing on the road makes you the bull in this china shop.

[Barnstable] has a policy of never accepting anything. As a happy consequence, it changes about as fast as the rules of chess.
— Kurt Vonnegut, "Where I Live"

Old King's Highway marker, Sandwich-Barnstable line. *Author's photo.*

Historical marker for the
West Parish of Barnstable.
Author's photo.

West Parish of Barnstable. *Author's photo.*

1) West Parish of Barnstable
2049 Meetinghouse Way,
West Barnstable, MA 02668
508 362-8624/4445
westparishmemorialfoundation.org
or www.westparish.org

Directions:
Very simply, from either end of the Cape, take Route 6 (the Mid-Cape Highway) to exit 5.

If you are coming from the west (Sandwich or the Cape Cod Canal), at the end of exit, turn left onto Meetinghouse Road. Drive 0.2 mile, over the highway. Look for the West Parish sign on your left, across from Church Street, and turn into the driveway. Park in the rear.

If you are coming from the east (Barnstable and the rest of the Cape), turn right at the end of the exit — look for the driveway 200 feet down on your left. Turn in and park in rear.

Description:
It is pretty apparent from the outside that this is the den of troublemakers. No, really. When the church was built, the congregation was already 100 years old. During that time, they had separated from the Church of England, been imprisoned, and finally exiled with their minister, Rev. John Lothrop. For the first 130 years, it also served as the center of town government and, for a time, as a school. The tower bell, cast by Paul Revere & Son, was a given in memory of Col. James Otis in 1806.

2) Old Parsonage & Lemuel Shaw Birthplace
410 Church Street, West Barnstable, MA
- Distance: 0.8 mile
- Driving Time: 3 minutes

Directions:
From the rear of the parking lot, drive down the hill behind the church, and turn right onto Cedar Street. Bear right, following the curve and keeping the church on the hill to your right. At the stop sign, cross Meetinghouse Road onto Church street, and continue to 410 Church Street. The stone monument will be on left. Pull off on onto the shoulder on your right. And please respect the private property here.

Old Parsonage & Lemuel Shaw Birthplace. *Author's photo.*

Sacrament Rock. *Author's photo.*

Description:

This was the home of Rev. Oakes Shaw, minister of the West Barnstable parish. His youngest son, Lemuel, was the quintessential American jurist for the first half of the 18ᵗʰ century, and the father-in-law of Herman Melville. As Massachusetts Chief Justice Shaw would have been hard to understand in modern times. He was strongly anti-slavery, but refused to free fugitive slaves in his custody. His decision supporting school segregation in Boston was the basis of the separate-but-equal rule, having himself grown up in an homogenous countryside. And while his decisions hampered worker's compensation law, he also acted to legitimize labor unions.

3) Sacrament Rock

2440 Main Street, West Barnstable, MA
- Distance: 2.4 miles
- Driving Time: 8 minutes

Directions:

Continue along Church Street for 0.1 miles, then bear left onto Parker Road. Continue on Parker Road for 0.7 miles, to the intersection with Route 6A. Bear left onto Route 6A (a/k/a Main Street) and drive for another 0.6 mile.

As you approach the intersection with Route 132, you will see a grass island in the road, heading uphill. The road bears to the left at the island, and you want to follow that. Route 132 bears off the right — do not take that. If you do take that wrong turn, you will know it when you see signs for Cape Cod Community College on your left. Turn around there before you get caught up in Hyannis-bound traffic.

Continuing along Route 6A/Main Street for 0.9 miles, watch for the entrance to West Barnstable Elementary School on your right. When you see it, park wherever is safest on either side of the road. The monument is on the opposite side of the road, and a few steps just up the hill.

Description:

Exiled from England to the Plymouth Bay Colony, Rev. John Lothrop led his congregation down from Scituate in 1639. Because only the northern part of the present-day town had been purchased from the local Mattakeese tribe at first, development pretty much was confined along Route 6A. Hence, Lothrop's congregation migrated to West Barnstable over the coming decades, taking their power with them. Considering that their first church here was a rock, anything would have been an improvement.

Lothrop Cemetery, Barnstable. *Author's photo.*

Daniel Davis House & Museum. *Author's photo.*

4) Lothrop Hill Cemetery

2440 Main Street, West Barnstable, MA
www.capecodgravestones.com/barnloth.html
- Distance: 0.7 miles
- Driving Time: 3 minutes

Directions:

Continue east along Route 6A/Main Street (the street numbers will be going down) for 0.7 miles. Look for a stone wall on your right, and the sign Lothrop Hill Cemetery. Again, find the safest spot on either side of the road to park.

Description:

Although Lothrop did seem to get around, he ended up not too far from his first place of worship in town. The graveyard also holds the tomb of colonial governor Thomas Hinckley, as well as the Cape's oldest gravestone, that of Dorothy Rawson from 1683. They've been burying people here for over 300 years, so it's a wonder that there's any room left.

5) Daniel Davis House & Museum

3074 Main Street, Barnstable, MA
508 362-2982
- Distance: 0.5 miles
- Driving Time: 2 minutes

Directions:

Continue east along Route 6A/Main Street for one half mile. On the right you will see St. Mary's Episcopal Church. Take the next driveway on your left, into the parking lot between the Daniel Davis House and Sturgis Library. After parking, walk back down to the street, turn right and look for the Davis House.

Description:

The headquarters for the Barnstable Historical Society was the home of Judge Daniel Davis and Mehitable Lothrop. It is maintained much the way it was in 1739, and shows how far those descendants of Rev. Lothrop's group had come in barely a hundred years.

Olde Colonial Courthouse. *Author's photo.*

Sturgis Library. *Author's photo.*

6) Olde Colonial Courthouse, Barnstable

Route 6A & Rendezvous Lane, Barnstable, MA
508 362-8927
www.talesofcapecod.org
- Distance: 400 feet
- Walking Time: 5 minutes

Directions:

From the front door of the Davis House, take a right and continue west on the sidewalk until you reach the intersection with Rendezvous Lane. The Courthouse will be the white clapboard building on your right.

Description:

Cape Cod on the verge of the American Revolution. When the British Crown taxes you without giving you a voice in government, you head up to Boston and dump subsidized imports into the harbor. When it appoints your governor rather than letting you elect him, you run him out of town. And two years after this courthouse was built, fifteen hundred people show up to keep the King's Court from sitting, in protest the revocation of the right to trial by jury. These days, Tales of Cape Cod, a local history group founded by Lou Cataldo, uses the building for a seasonal lecture series and other special events on topics like "The New England Vampire Tradition".

7) Sturgis Library

3090 Main Street, Barnstable, MA
508 362-6636
www.sturgislibrary.org
- Distance: 550 feet
- Walking Time: 5 minutes

Directions:

Returning to Route 6A, take a left up the sidewalk, in the direction you just came. Continue past the driveway you parked in, to the sign in front of the Sturgis Library.

Crocker Tavern. *Author's photo.*

Description:

Not only does the place still have Rev. Lothrop's 1605 bible, but the very front was Lothrop's home, built in 1644. It eventually passed to his descendant, William Sturgis, who made his fortune beginning at age 15 in the northwest Pacific fur trade. Upon his death in 1863, he bequeathed the home as a library — Lemuel Shaw was named one of the first trustees.

On a personal note, it was in the library's Kitteredge Maritime Collection room that I drew inspiration for my first novel about Sturgis' forbearer, Captain John Kendrick of South Orleans, commander of the first American expedition around the world.

8) Crocker Tavern

3095 Main St, Barnstable, MA
508 362-4090
www.crockertavern.com
• Distance: 100 feet
• Walking Time: 1 minutes

Directions:

Continue just a little further up the street, and look for the dark clapboard house on the opposite side of the street.

Description:

In Revolutionary days, Aunt Lydia's Tavern (named for Lydia Crocker Sturgis) was the center of Patriot activity, led by James Otis, Jr. It is not hard to believe that a bar across the street from a courthouse would foment government subversion. It had already been around a couple decades when local minutemen gathered there before marching off to action in Bunker Hill and the siege of Boston. It has been restored and is now a vacation rental.

Mercy Otis Warren.
Author's photo.

James Otis, Jr. *Author's photo.*

9) Barnstable County Superior Courthouse
3195 Main Street, Barnstable
508 362-4090
www.barnstablecounty.org
• Distance: 0.2 miles
• Driving Time: 2 minutes

Directions:
Returning to your car, exit the driveway for the library by turning left onto Route 6A/Main Street. Go up the hill and back down again — hardly 1,000 feet. Look for the first parking place on your right, below the hill with the courthouse above. Take either set of steps to the front entrance.

Description:
To get a sense of how local government works in Massachusetts, you should first realize that Barnstable County (all of Cape Cod) was founded in 1685. Now recall that Rev. Lothrop's people founded the Town of Barnstable in 1639. Sandwich is even older. County government is the newcomer and never has had the power or respect that the towns do.

That aside, this is one of my favorite spots on the Cape. If you grab a sandwich down the hill in Barnstable village, bring it up here, find a place on the steps, and look out to the Barnstable Harbor and Sandy Neck in the distance.

Lou Cataldo, local historian from down the street, is most responsible for the statues of dueling Otises. To one side, Mercy Otis Warren, poet, playwright, an ardent advocate for the education of women and American independence, merciless in her attacks against Loyalist officials.

On the other side, her older brother, attorney James Otis, Jr., stands in a pose he might have taken in Boston 1760, arguing against the British government's power to enter and occupy any colonist's home. Always persuasive, in later life he told Mercy that his preferred method of dying would be by lightning. A few months before the signing of peace with England, Otis got his wish, being struck by lightning in 1783. Defense attorney's take note.

Wood "Gaol." *Author's photo.*

Coast Guard Heritage Museum. *Author's photo.*

10) Coast Guard Heritage Museum
3353 Main Street, Barnstable, MA 02630
508 362-8521
• Distance: 0.3 miles
• Driving Time: 2 minutes

Directions:
Continue east on Route 6A/Main Street, through Barnstable Village. When you reach the stop light, go straight and up the hill. Look for the red brick museum on your right, and take your first right into the driveway.

Description:
When a packet or schooner would arrive in Barnstable Harbor, the captain's first duty would be to trudge up Cobbs Hill to the Customs House. Built in 1856, it later served at the U.S. Post Office, and now houses the U.S. Coast Guard Heritage Museum — another labor of love by Lou Cataldo and Tales of Cape Cod. Next door, the original 1690s wood jail (or "gaol"), sports carvings from inmates going back to the 17th century.

Iyanough Burial Site. *Author's photo.*

11) Iyanough Burial Site
4030 Main Street, Cummaquid, MA 02637
- Distance: 1.3 miles
- Driving Time: 2 minutes

Directions:
Continue east on Route 6A/Main Street for 1.3 miles. Watch for the Cummaquid Post Office on your right. Find the safest place to park on either side of the road. The marker is 150 feet further east across from the post office. Next to it is a lane that leads down to the site.

Description:
We can stop talking about dead white men for a moment. Iyanough was the Sachem of the Mattakeese village of Wompanoag, who welcomed the Pilgrims as friends. Variations of his name are found around Barnstable in "Hyannis" and "Wianno." His son, John Hyano, having died, Iyanough's granddaughter, Mary, came to live with him. Tradition had it that the Wampanoag had intermarried with white men who had come much earlier, possibly the Vikings. This would account for the tall stature and fair complexion of the Wampanoag at the time.

As it happened, a Gypsy exiled from England, Austin Bearse, was sent down the Barnstable upon his arrival in Plymouth. Considered an unattractive suitor (neither English nor Congregationalist), Austin instead married the red-haired Mary Wampanoag. Their descendants include Ambrose Bierce and the 42 and 44th Presidents of the United States, father and son George Bush, which puts a completely different spin on Thanksgiving at the White House.

Yet again, we have Lou Cataldo and Tales of Cape Cod to thank for preserving the site.

Hallet's Store.
Author's photo.

Old King's Highway marker: Yarmouth-Barnstable line.
Author's photo.

Faith S. Tufts Gate House at the Old Yarmouth Nature Trails.
Author's photo.

12) Hallet's Store
139 Main Street, Yarmouthport, MA
508-362-3362
www.hallets.com
- Distance: 1.4 miles
- Driving Time: 3 minutes

Directions:
Continue east on Route 6A/Main Street for 0.8 miles. On your right, you will see the official state highway marker "Entering Yarmouth." On opposite sides of the road will also be stone markers unique to Route 6A.

Continue another 0.6 miles and watch for the sign on the right for Hallet's Store. Parking is on the right side of the street.

Old King's Highway marker: Barnstable-Yarmouth line. *Author's photo.*

Description:
Reeking of Americana, Hallet's was a pharmacy with a lunch counter. No more pharmacy, but if you've made it this far, treat yourself to an ice cream soda. And check out the Hallet Museum upstairs — the place has been in the family for four generations. Open seasonally for breakfast and lunch.

13) Old Yarmouth Nature Trails
229 Main Street, Yarmouth Port, MA
508-362-3362
www.hsoy.org
- Distance: 0.3 miles
- Driving Time: 1 minute

Directions:
Continue east on Route 6A/Main Street for 0.3 miles. Look on the right for the sign for the Historical Society of Old Yarmouth. The driveway is just before the entrance to the Yarmouth Port Post Office. Drive past the small white Gorham Cobbler Shop on your right, and park on the shoulder, opposite the Gate House.

Description:
Okay, now you can leave the car for a while. Please observe the sign at the gate house and leave fifty cents in the box. Trails snake through the fifty acres of wood here (formerly the first golf course on the Cape), but if you're feeling like ambling, take care for ticks, even in the off-season.

Kelley Chapel. *Author's photo.*

Captain Bangs Hallet House. *Author's photo.*

14) Kelley Chapel
- Distance: 400 feet
- Walking Time: 5 minutes

Directions:
Take the gravel trail to the left of the Gate House and continue straight to the two buildings in the clearing.

Description:
The Kelleys were Quakers, and erected the chapel in 1873 following the death of a child, intending it for the use of the poor of South Yarmouth. It was moved here in the 1960s. Although normally not open, it is often is rented out for weddings, and hosts an ecumenical service on Thanksgiving.

15) Captain Bangs Hallet House
11 Strawberry Lane, Yarmouth Port
508 362-3021
www.hsoy.org
- Distance: 800 feet
- Walking Time: 8 minutes

Directions:
Return back to the Gate House, and take the paved way that bears off to the right and up the hill. You will be entering the Hallet House from the rear. Look for the large tree on your right.

Description:
Before you enter the house, don't miss the weeping beech you passed on the way in. Under the canopy of the tree, it feels like some kind of Gothic novel.

You've driven by many sea captain's homes, now it's time to actually go in one. If practical, try get here for a tour. The place is restored to the way Anna Hallet kept it while her husband was off one some lengthy adventure on the other side of the world. From the look of the furnishings, it was worth it at the time. Open seasonally through the fall.

Edward Gorey House. *Author's photo.*

New Church,
Yarmouth Port.
Author's photo.

16) Edward Gorey House

8 Strawberry Lane, Yarmouth Port
508 362-3909
www.edwardgoreyhouse.org
• Distance: 200 feet
• Walking Time: 2 minutes

Directions:

From the front of the Hallet House, cross Strawberry Lane, keeping the park on your left.

Description:

Remember the weeping beech tree? It is tailor-made for an Edward Gorey scene. There's a small fee for entering his house, but the tour is self-guided. Gorey's genius is easily recognizable in his plays, books, and, of course, illustrations.

17) New Church

262 Main Street, Yarmouth Port, MA
508 362-3909
• Distance: 400 feet
• Walking Time: 3 minutes

Directions:

From the front of the Gorey House, either take a right down Strawberry Lane or cross the park to Route 6A. At the front of the park is a crosswalk directly from the church. Cross 6A to the sidewalk opposite.

Description:

The Church of the New Jerusalem, known as the Swedenborgians, separated from the Congregationalists (who, 200 years earlier, were themselves known as Separatists from the Church of England). Before this church was built in 1870, they met on the second floor of the Parnassus Books building, just one block down. Their numbers dwindling, the building is now being preserved by the Yarmouth New Church Preservation Foundation.

Winslow Crocker House. *Author's photo.*

Taylor-Bray Farm. *Author's photo.*

18) Winslow Crocker House
250 Route 6A, Yarmouth Port
508 375-9183
www.historicnewengland.org
• Distance: 300 feet
• Walking Time: 2 minutes

Directions:
Facing Route 6A from the front of the New Church, take a right and follow the sidewalk to the stone wall on your right. The Crocker House is set well back from the road.

Description:
Built in 1780 in West Barnstable by Winslow Crocker, it showed Cape Codders could still make money during the Revolutionary War. Mary Thacher moved the house here in 1936 (pretty much along the route you just came), next to another she owned, and proceeded to fill it with her vast collection of antiques. It is now run by Historic New England, and open seasonally.

19) Taylor-Bray Farm
108 Bray Farm Road North, Yarmouth
www.taylorbrayfarm.org
• Walking Distance (back to car): 700 feet
• Walking Time: 3 minutes
• Driving Distance: 3.2 miles
• Driving Time: 8 minutes

Directions:
Continue west along the sidewalk and cross the street at the post office. Follow the driveway for the Historical Society back to where you parked near the Gate House.

Exiting out of the driveway, take a right onto Route 6A. Head east for 2.7 miles and watch for Oliver's Restaurant on your left. Turn left onto Bray Farm Road (a/k/a Bray Farm Road South) and follow for 0.4 miles. As the road forks and narrows, bear right, then pull off to the left and park to right of the barn.

Description:

Richard Taylor set his home down here in this pasture next to the Hockanom marsh in 1639. But the story goes that a thousand years ago Leif Erikson's brother, Thorwald, was buried in a nearby hill after being killed in a battle with the "Skraellings" (as the Vikings called the natives). In 1896, the Bray brothers bought the farm from the Taylor family and, while living there, kept a large semi-domesticated snake under the floorboards (shades of Edward Gorey).

The Town of Yarmouth bought the 22 acre farm in 1987, and the Taylor-Bray Farm Preservation Association took over management and preservation in 2001. You can visit the place year-round, picnic, walk the paths, or meet the animals, including the Scottish Highland Cattle (who may bear a passing resemblance to old Thorwald).

Scotty and Fiona, Scottish Highland Cattle, Taylor-Bray Farm. *Author's photo.*

Old King's Highway marker: Dennis-Yarmouth line. *Author's photo.*

We liked Dennis well, better than any town we had seen on the Cape...
– Henry David Thoreau, *Cape Cod*

20) 1736 Josiah Dennis Manse Museum
77 Nobscusset Rd, Dennis
508 385-2232
www.dennishistsoc.org
- Distance: 2.2 miles
- Driving Time: 6 minutes

Old King's Highway marker: Yarmouth-Dennis line. *Author's photo.*

Directions:
Turn around and follow Bray Farm Road back out to Route 6A. Take a left onto Route 6A, heading east. On your right, you will see the official state highway marker "Entering Dennis." Again, opposite sides of the road will feature the stone markers for distances to Plymouth and Provincetown.

Drive for 1.8 miles on Route 6A, then take a left onto Nobscusset Road, just after the grass island at the intersection with New Boston Road. Keeping the playground on your left, continue up Nobscusset for 0.3 miles and look for the driveway for the Josiah Dennis Manse on your left, at the corner with Whig Street.

Description:
When the town of Dennis split off from Yarmouth in 1793, it honored the first minister of the area, Rev. Josiah Dennis, by taking his name. The town now owns his house, built 1736, and the adjacent 1745 Schoolhouse. If you manage to get here at the right time, a costumed docent will guide you through the house. Take special note of the diorama of the Shiverick Shipyard.

1736 Josiah Dennis Manse Museum. *Author's photo.*

Cape Cod Museum of the Arts. *Author's pho*

Cape Playhouse. *Author's pho*

21) Cape Cod Center for the Arts

60 Hope Lane, Dennis
508 385-4477
www.capecodcenterforthearts.org
www.ccmoa.org
www.capecinema.com
www.capeplayhouse.com
- Distance: 0.6 mile
- Driving Time: 2 minutes

Directions:

Exit the driveway and turn right onto Whig Street. Continue through the intersection with Nobscusset Road, and take the next right onto Hope Lane. Follow Hope Lane for 0.2 miles, then take a left into the driveway for the Cape Cod Center for the Arts.

The Cape Cod Museum of the Arts will be directly to your left. If you want to immediately continue on, the Cape Cinema will be next on your left. You can then follow the driveway to the sign for the Cape Playhouse. Park at ticket booth to the right of the Playhouse front entrance.

Description:

Since Cape Cod became a summer resort area at the beginning of the 1900s, some of those visitors have been pining for more than sand dunes and salt sea air. This whole complex is a testament to that desire. Paintings, sculpture, art house films, live theater — even a café. I'm not going to begin to give the history here, except to say you should definitely mark your map and come back for in the evening for an exhibition or a show.

Scargo Tower. *Author's photo*

Looking north from Scargo Tower. *Author's photo.*

22) Scargo Tower
152 Scargo Hill Rd, Dennis, MA 02638
508 394-8300
www.town.dennis.ma.us
- Distance: 0.9 mile
- Driving Time: 3 minutes

Directions:
Continue around the driveway in front of the Playhouse to the exit onto Route 6A. You will see the stone road marker on your left. Take a right onto Route 6A west. Drive 0.2 miles, then take a left onto Old Bass River Road.

Drive up the hill for 0.2 miles, then bear left onto Scargo Hill Road. Continue for 0.6 miles, and watch on the left for a sign for Scargo Tower (do not confuse with Scargo Heights Road). Take a left up the hill, and park on the right, beyond the tower.

Description:
There have been three towers up here, one of the highest points on the Cape. The first in 1874, made of wood, blew down. The second, also made of wood, burned down in 1900. The third, this one made of cobblestone, was built in 1901.

This is one spot that is better in the winter. Although 30 feet tall, the trees are creeping up around it, and the summer view, while great, is partially obscured. From November to April, you can see from Cape Cod Bay to Nantucket Sound, and across to the Pilgrim Monument in Provincetown.

Shiverick Shipyard monument. *Author's photo.*

Sesuit Harbor. *Author's photo.*

Harborview Beach. *Author's photo.*

23) Shiverick Shipyard Monument
Sesuit Neck Road, East Dennis
- Distance: 2 miles
- Driving Time: 7 minutes

Directions:
Drive out of the tower parking lot. At the bottom of the hill, turn left onto Scargo Hill Road and continue for 0.6 miles.

At the intersection with Route 6A, bear right. Continue on Route 6A for 0.4 miles, to the stop lights at Route 134.

Turn left onto Bridge Road, and take it for 0.3 miles to the intersection with Sesuit Neck Road.

Turn right onto Sesuit Neck Road and drive for 0.5 miles. Off to your right and below will be Sesuit Harbor — watch for the monument facing the road. You can try to pull off the road or park in the lot just below and walk up.

Description:
Now recall that diorama from the Dennis Manse. Asa Shiverick started building ships here in 1815. He needed fairly deep water, but still protected, to build anything sizeable. Sesuit Harbor fit the bill, and when the California Gold rush began, Shiverick's sons were well-positioned to produce the ocean greyhounds — the clipper ships. As you look down the hill, you'll see dozens and dozens of sport fishing and pleasure boats that now call this home.

24) Harborview Beach
Harbor Road, East Dennis
- Distance: 0.3 miles
- Driving Time: 1 minute

Directions:
Depending upon the time of year and time of day, you may choose leave this off the tour or to walk this last leg. If it is the early afternoon of a beautiful summer day, the small lot at Harborview Beach is restricted to residents only. Any other time of year, or even late afternoon/early evening in the summer, parking is not at a premium.

Either way, getting there is no problem. Continue on Sesuit Neck Road, as it bears left away from the marina. The road's name changes to Harbor Road here. Watch for the small parking lot on your right.

Description:
Hopefully, you don't need to be told what to do at a beach. If you kept your eye on your watch, and arrived here just before sunset, grab a comfortable patch of sand — or walk out on the jetty — to see if you can catch a glimpse of the cliffs of Manomet, just south of Plymouth. You get an idea why the Mattakeese, the Vikings, and the Pilgrims all chose to settle here. Not a bad way to end an odyssey.

Woods Hole. *Courtesy of Cape Cod Aerial Photography.*

"View of Woods Hole village from harbor hill, about 1880."
Courtesy of NEFSC Photo Archives.

Walk or Bike Tour 3

Old Salts and Oceanographers

Woods Hole

Overall Distance: Walking 1.12 miles, Driving/Biking 5.1 miles

Time: 3 hours

Public Restrooms: Woods Hole ferry terminal, Woods Hole Library, and every government building (but typically closed on weekends)

Note: Woods Hole, like Chatham and Provincetown, is the end of the road. The only difference is here is that it is also a jumping off point to Martha's Vineyard. So a mass of humanity, vehicles, and cargo come on down the road, get on the ferry, and bypass the village for the most part. It really wasn't much of a place at all until the 1870s, when federal fisheries officials set up shop. That drew scientists, and then research vessels… and more scientists… and more federal and private dollars… followed by some philanthropists who decided to summer here, too.

Best advice: Call the MBL or WHOI and arrange to take a tour. Then plan your time around that.

Getting there: If you can help it, don't take your car into Woods Hole unless it is the dead of winter. And really don't try to drive there on a Friday afternoon, when everyone is trying to get their car on the Martha's Vineyard ferry. But if you must drive, take a pocket full of quarters. The meters are hard to come by and don't last too long on 25 cents.

Falmouth Bus Station. *Author's photo.*

Shining Sea Bikeway. *Author's photo*

Woods Hole Steamship Authority Terminal. *Author's photo.*

Falmouth Bus Station
The Sealine and the WHOOSH trolley
15 minutes from Falmouth to Woods Hole
800 352-7155
www.thebreeze.info

Walking: Take the bus. Now, here is where things get a little stupid. The transit authority runs buses from Hyannis to Woods Hole in the winter, and a separate summer shuttle from Falmouth to Woods Hole — that's not the stupid part. But if you actually arrive from off-Cape by bus, into the Falmouth Bus station, you need to call the shuttle for a pickup — the bus station is not a regular bus stop.

Now, if you are not coming in by bus, then find your way to the Falmouth Mall on Route 28 and park there. The bus will pick up in front of the big clock.

Bike: If you have a bike, take it. The Shining Sea Bikeway begins at the Falmouth Bus station, but the parking lot is a little further along. Continue down Route 28, then turn right at the fork onto Locust Road. Look on the right for signs for the bikeway. The bikeway follows the old railroad bed for 3.6 miles, running parallel Vineyard Sound for some breathtaking views.

By either bike or bus, you'll end up in front of the Steamship Authority's Wood Hole Terminal. If you want to tack on a trip to Vineyard, the schedule can be found at www. steamshipauthority.com or by calling 508 548-3788.

Important: Bring a government-issued photo ID. You'll need it for the aquarium.

Woods Hole Historical Museum. *Author's photo.*

Swift Boat Barn.
Author's photo

1) Woods Hole Historical Museum
579 Woods Hole Road,
    Woods Hole, MA 02543
508 548-7270
www.woodsholemuseum.org
- Distance: 550 feet
- Time: 4 minutes

Directions:
    With your back to the ferry terminal, take Railroad Avenue up the hill to Woods Hole Road. Cross the street, take a right and follow the sidewalk past the library. The museum is the next door down.

Description:
    My favorite part of the museum is the scale model of the Woods Hole from 1895, with the railroad. Since you don't come to Woods Hole unless you're drawn to the water, the Swift Barn holds a variety of small boats and sailing pennants. A small boat building and restoration program is located to the rear of the barn.

Woods Hole Historical Museum. *Author's photo*

WHOI Ocean Science Exhibit Center. *Author's photo.*

2) WHOI Ocean Science Exhibit Center

15 School Street, Woods Hole, MA 02543
(508) 289-2663 or (508) 289-2700
www.whoi.edu
- Distance: 850 feet
- Walking Time: 7 minutes

Directions:

Leaving the museum, turn right on Woods Hole Road. As the road bears to the right, it becomes Water Street. Follow it 300 feet to School Street. Turn right onto School Street and walk another 300 feet. Look for the white building on your right.

Description:

I never took a chemistry class in high school. Instead, our science teacher, Michael DiSpezio, somehow managed to convince the powers-that-be to allow him to teach an oceanography class. As this was much more applied science in a lab located in my backyard, it was much easier to grasp. We were always talking about the Alvin, too. At the time, WHOI was producing stunning films about what its deep sea submersible was finding in hydrothermic vents three miles undersea. Of course, we were probably more interested in how Alvin helped retrieve a hydrogen bomb from a sunken U.S. submarine in the 1960s. And then there's the discovery of the Titanic in 1986.

Angelus Tower.
Author's photo.

3) Angelus Tower & Garden of Our Lady
St. Joseph's Church
Millfield Street, Woods Hole, MA 02543
508 508-289-7423
www.whoi.edu
  • Distance: 0.33 miles
  • Walking Time: 12 minutes

Directions:
From the WHOI center, turn right on School Street. Follow it for 900 feet, past the school and Eel Pond. Turn left on Millfield Street, and continue for 700 feet until you come to the tower and the garden entrance on the left.

Description:
One might assume an incongruity here, with this religious monument among all these eggheads. It was the idea of one those scientists, actually. Frances Crane Lillie studied at the Marine Biological Laboratory in 1894. She married Frank R. Lillie, who was to become president of MBL. She gave the tower in 1929 in hopes that the tolling of its bells would be a reminder to the local scientific community of the presence of God.

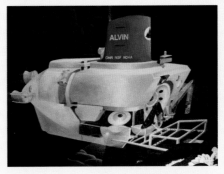

Mural of the *DSV Alvin*.
Author's photo.

Eel Pond. *Author's photo.*

Woods Hole Science Aquarium. *Author's photo.*

Woods Hole
Science
Aquarium,
touch tanks.
Author's photo

4) Woods Hole Science Aquarium
10 Albatross Street, Woods Hole, MA
508 495-2001
aquarium.nefsc.noaa.gov
• Distance: 0.25 miles
• Walking Time: 10 minutes

Directions:
From the tower, turn left on Millfield Street and continue for 600 feet. Turn left onto Albatross Street and walk another 600 feet. The aquarium is the large brick building on the left.

Description:
The aquarium is free, but you need a government-issued photo ID to get in. It's a federal building, after all, in the offices of the National Marine Fisheries Service. If you're going to study fish, you might want to bring a few back to the office alive. There's been a research aquarium in Woods Hole since 1885. You'll find a seal exhibit out front, plenty of fish swimming on display inside, and a touch tank upstairs. Just remember to be gentle with the creatures there — for the most part, they're not very fearsome.

Hammerhead shark, Woods Hole Science Aquarium. *Author's photo.*

Yalden Sundial and Waterfront. *Author's photo.*

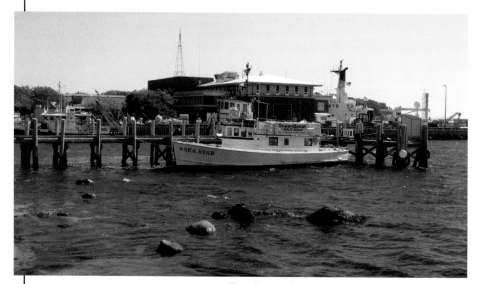

The OceanQuest's *Sea Star*. *Author's photo.*

5) Yalden Sundial
Waterfront Park
Water Street, Woods Hole, MA 02543
- Distance: 600 feet
- Walking Time: 5 minutes

Directions:
From the aquarium, turn left on Albatross Street. As the street hooks to the left, it becomes Water Street. Follow the sidewalk along the water for 450 feet. Look for the park on your right.

Description:
Check your watch. The Yalden sundial is purported to be accurate to within 30 seconds. It was a gift of Ambassador Charles R. Crane, in 1937. This past president of MBL, so connected to the environment, a few years earlier had played a major role in the opening up Saudi Arabian fields to American oil companies.

Looking across the water, you can see some of the closer Elizabeth Islands. These extend in a southwesterly direction from the Cape and are very sparsely populated. The largest, Naushon, is owned by a trust controlled by the Forbes family (including Senator John Forbes Kerry). The eight square-mile island has about only 30 houses and one pickup truck. There's a working farm with sheep and cows, and people (visiting family members and the help) get about on foot or by horseback. It is probably the best example of what Cape Cod may have looked like a century or two ago — thus showing that only the truly wealthy can afford to live primitively.

6) Vessels
Waterfront Park
Water Street
Woods Hole, MA 02543
- Distance: 120 feet
- Walking Time: 1 minute

Directions:
From the sundial, continue along the harbor keeping the water on your right. Look for the piers on your right.

WHOI's *R/V Tioga. Author's photo.*

Pierce Visitors Center, Marine Biological Laboratory. *Author's photo.*

Sea Star
www.oceanquest.org
800 376-2326

Description:
Oceanquest was just the sort of thing we tried to do, ad hoc, when Mr. DiSpezio was teaching us teenagers. Besides special charters and school trips, they run a 90-minute educational cruise on the *Sea Star* for the general public in the summer. Real hands-on oceanography, gathering sea life and studying it on board. As this is a shorter walking tour, check out their schedule and consider adding on this side trip.

R/V Tioga
www.whoi.edu/page.do?pid=8159

Description:
WHOI maintains a fleet of research ships, many that travel the globe. If you're lucky, you may be able to catch the larger ones in their home port. Unlike the deep-diving *Alvin*, *Tioga* is a small, swift vessel, used mostly for a diversity of day trips along the coast, including tagging and tracking Right Whales.

7) Marine Biological Laboratory
Pierce Visitors Center
100 Water Street, Woods Hole, MA
www.mbl.edu
- Distance: 190 feet
- Walking Time: 1 minute

Directions:
Return to Water Street, take a right and follow the sidewalk. The visitors center is the next building down.

Description:
Besides a gift shop, the exhibits at the visitors center show you what MBL, a private teaching and research institution, has been doing in Woods Hole since 1888. And, more importantly, how their work directly affects your life.

The Candle House. Marine Biological Laboratory. *Author's photo.*

Entrance to the Candle House. *Author's photo.*

The Candle House. *Author's photo.*

8) The Candle House

127 Water Street, Woods Hole, MA 02543
508 289-7623
www.mbl.edu
• Distance: 50 feet
• Walking Time: 1 minute

Directions:

From the MBL visitors center, cross the street to the large stone building.

Directions:

Good for you if you called ahead for a tour. They take an hour and run twice a day. The Candle House, built in 1836, was originally used to store whale oil. Before the feds and the MBL came to town, Woods Hole thrived on whaling and guano fertilizer. The odor of whale rendering and the fertilizer probably kept the tourists away.

MBL is where Mr. DiSpezio worked as a research assistant in the 1970s, before coming to teach us goofballs. It's pretty easy to see why the place has been on the cutting edge of research for over 100 years, producing 49 Nobel Laureates. And one great science educator.

Woods Hole, Water Street, 1845. *Courtesy of NEFSC Photo Archives.*

WHOI Information Office. *Author's photo.*

Old Stone Bridge looking towards Great Harbor. *Author's photo.*

9) WHOI Information Office

93 Water Street, Woods Hole, MA 02543
508 289-2252
www.whoi.edu
- Distance: 175 feet
- Walking Time: 1 minute

Directions:

From the Candle House, continue down the north side of Water Street.

Description:

If you passed on the MBL tour, then try the one given by WHOI. They are given twice daily in the summer. You may also want to see if you can sign up any errant teenagers for a long research voyage to the Indian Ocean.

10) Old Stone Bridge

Water Street, Woods Hole, MA 02543
- Distance: 265 feet
- Walking Time: 1 minute

Directions:

From the WHOI info office, continue along Water Street to the bridge.

Description:

Besides being a working drawbridge (research vessels sometimes enter through here and dock in Eel Pond), this is the start of the Falmouth Road Race, which attracts thousand of runners. From here you can also get an idea of how narrow the channel is, being a chokepoint between Buzzards Bay and Vineyard Sound. When bringing a sailboat with an overheating engine through here in 1997, I had timed it poorly and was set against the tide. It pulls so strongly through here that the tall channel buoys are pulled almost horizontal. It took us over an hour to go a half mile.

Approaching Nobska Light. *Author's photo.*

Nobska Light and Keepers House. *Author's photo*

11) Nobska light
Nobska Road, Woods Hole, MA 02543
508-457-3219
www.lighthouse.cc/nobska
• Distance: 1.1 miles
• Biking Time: 15 minutes

Directions:
If you're on foot, return to the bus stop and ferry dock by walking down Water Street, taking a left onto Luscombe Ave and walking to the end.

Driving or Biking: Continue down Water Street, and up the hill past the library and historical museum on your left. After another quarter mile, turn right onto Church Street. Follow Church Street for another ¾ mile down to the end. Parking is on the left.

Description:
Because of the narrow passage, the whaling fleet based in Woods Hole in the 1800s needed a beacon to guide their way home. The first light here was installed in 1829, and was replaced with the one you see here in 1876. Over the next hundred years, it was renovated a number of times, and then automated in 1985.

You can see why this is where the Falmouth Road Race ends. There's a commanding view of Vineyard Sound and Naushon Island. The Coast Guard commander for southeast New England has the lighthouse keeper's home to stay in. The tower is opened in a limited basis, so call ahead for hours.

The Conant House. *Author's photo.*

Julia Wood House. *Author's photo.*

Side Trip
Falmouth Green

Distance: 0.8 miles
Time: 1-1.5 hours
Public Restrooms: Falmouth Historical Society, Falmouth
Town Hall

Either going to or coming from Woods Hole, an easy and convenient side-trip is visiting the area surround the Village Green in Falmouth.

1) The Conant House
65 Palmer Ave

Directions
From the Falmouth Bus Depot, take a left onto Depot Ave. and walk 500 feet down to Route 28. Take a left on Route 28, walk 350 feet and cross. Directly ahead is Palmer Avenue — follow it for 500 feet, and cross the street. The Conant House will be on your left.

Description
Built in 1760, the rendering pots on the lawn are an indication of the reminders of Falmouth's whaling history inside.

2) Julia Wood House & Hallett Barn
55 Palmer Avenue
508-548-4857
www.falmouthhistoricalsociety.org

Directions
From the front of the Conant House, turn left and continue past the garden to the yellow house, just next door. Before entering the Julia Wood House, proceed to the Hallett Barn, just to the rear.

Description
The barn holds the real hands-on exhibits, while the Wood house gives a good picture of life in antebelleum New England. Don't miss the various gardens surrounding it all.

Village Green.
Author's photo.

First Congregational
Church of Falmouth.
Author's photo.

Mostly Hall. *Author's photo.*

3) First Congregational Church of Falmouth
68 Main Street
508 548-3700
www.firstcongfalmouth.org

Directions
From the Wood House, turn left onto Palmer Ave. Keep the green on your right. The church is a few doors down on your left.

Description
Founded 1708 as a branch of the Barnstable church, this building was originally built in 1796 across the green, then moved here in 1857. A year later, William Bates became the minister here, but he died in 1859, leaving a wife and five young children in the parsonage just up the street.

4) Village Green
Palmer Avenue, Hewins & West Main Streets

Directions
From the church, cross Palmer Ave to enter the green.

Description
Quintessential New England, the green is the site of numerous community activities throughout the year, including the start of the Cape Cod Marathon in October.

5) Mostly Hall
27 West Main Street
508 548-3786
www.mostlyhall.com

Directions
From the flagpole, head away from the church, to the opposite corner of the green. Cross Hewins Street, then West Main and take a right, following the sidewalk to the large green house on your left.

Description
Built in a southern style for his South Carolina bride in 1849, Albert Nye's Mostly Hall ushered in an era of the wealthy summer visitors that has yet to abate. Note: This is private property.

6) Katharine Lee Bates Birthplace
16 West Main Street

Directions
Cross West Main Street and continue down to #16, which is a white colonial on your right.

Description
Katharine Lee Bates's father was the new minister up the street at the Congregational Church when she was born here in the summer of 1859. He died a month later, and the family moved around Falmouth before settling in Wellesley, outside Boston. She continued to visit Falmouth annually, but it was during a trip from Chicago to Colorado in 1893 that she penned "America the Beautiful."

To return:
Continue along West Main to Route Route 28. Take a right and walk 250 feet. Cross Route 28, and walk back up Depot Ave to the Falmouth Bus Depot.

Katharine Lee Bates birthplace. *Author's photo.*

Chatham. *Courtesy of Cape Cod Aerial Photography.*

Chatham Railroad at the bend.
From a private collection.

Chatham Spur of the Cape Cod Rail
Trail. *Author's photo.*

Elbow Land

Chatham

You don't pass through Chatham. You have to intend to go there. At the elbow of the Cape, protected by barrier beaches, the town is surrounded on three sides by water. Sixteen square miles within 72 miles of coastline. The Route 6 Mid-Cape Highway bypasses it. Route 28 comes into town, then hangs a dogleg and takes you right out again. Many drivers will have that lost look on their face, and claim they knew they were in Chatham… but somehow got themselves to Orleans or Harwich. Because Chatham is off the beaten path, it has managed to maintain the character that other downtowns lost in the sixties, seventies, and eighties.

The railroad came to Chatham later than the rest of the Cape — 1887, and may not have come at all if it hadn't been for wealthy brewer Marcellus Eldredge. It was a dead-end for the line, and a curve to the south just before arriving in town led to several derailments into the sand banks by overzealous engineers. Discontinued after only 50 years, I've heard the rails were torn up and sold to Japan prior to World War II. When the state created the Rail Trail bike path, on the bed of the old line, Chatham again dragged its feet for twenty years before bringing it to town. By two wheels is the best way to see the place (but watch the sand on those curves).

Distance: 7 miles
Time: 4.5 hours
Public Restrooms: Veteran's Field, Eldredge Public Library, Chatham Town Offices, Kate Gould Park (seasonally), Lighthouse Beach (seasonally), Monomoy Wildlife Refuge (seasonally), Chase Park (seasonally), Chatham Fish Pier
Note: This is my home town, and I've always told people that Chatham is a bunch of circles. You really can't get too lost since you'll always end up running into the water or back where you started. You can follow a big circle around, or bisect the circle and cut across through the center. This route takes both approaches, and makes a figure-8. But don't be afraid of investigating any side roads. You won't be lost for long.

1) Chatham Railroad Museum
153 Depot Rd, Chatham, MA
508 945-5175
www.chathamrailroadmuseum.com

Directions:
Most people arrive into Chatham on Route 28 (Main Street) from Harwich and/or Route 6. As you enter Chatham, you will come to stop lights at a 5-road intersection, with the white Unitarian Universalist Meeting House on the hill before you. Bear left onto Depot Road (not a harder left onto Crowell Road) and continue up the hill. A few hundred feet after Post Office Road, you will see Veteran's Field below on your right, and the fire station and elementary school on your left. The Railroad Museum is just after the school. Parking is in front of the museum, or, when school is out, adjacent and behind the school.

Description:
Going to the elementary school just next door, I loved going to the Railroad Museum whenever it was open. The building was given to the town in 1951 and opened as a museum in 1961 (a typically deliberate Chatham pace). There's a model of what the whole rail yard used to look like, and the clicking of the telegraph can be heard from the station master's office. Visiting the 1910 New York Central caboose is real treat for kids, letting them imagine what life on the rails would have been like a century ago.

Chatham Railroad Museum.
Author's photo.

Chatham Town Team, 1920s.
From a private collection.

2) Veteran's Field

Depot Road & Veteran's Field Road, Chatham
www.chathamas.com
- Distance: 500 feet
- Walking Time: 2 minutes

Directions:

Cross Depot Road to the stairs down to playground. Walk up the hill to the bleachers behind home plate.

Description:

Summer baseball goes back at least a hundred year in Chatham. When a German U-boat started shelling Orleans in World War I, the crews of the Naval Air station based in Chathamport were playing the town team way — and they had to rush back over three miles and get their torpedo planes off the ground. The Cape Summer League boasts the best in college talent from around the country, and was featured in the movie, "Summer Catch."

Veteran's Field. *Author's photo.*

First Congregational
Church of Chatham.
Author's photo.

Sears Park.
Author's photo.

Nickerson Monument.
Author's photo.

3) Sears Park

Main Street & Seaview Street, Chatham, MA
- Distance: 0.3 miles
- Walking Time: 10 minutes

Directions:

From the hill behind home plate, walk down the hill towards the back of the community center, keeping the little league field on your left. Follow the driveway out of the community center to Main Street. Take a left and follow the sidewalk to the rotary. Cross Old Harbor Road, towards the Congregational Church.

Continue east on Main Street, passing the church on your left, for another 600 feet. Look for the small triangular park with the obelisk at the intersection with Seaview Street.

Description:

More than 10% of the whole population of Chatham went off to the Civil War, referred more accurately on this obelisk as "the Rebellion." These few never made it home. Please keep in mind this is a memorial park — town by-Laws do not permit its use as a playground or picnic area.

4) Nickerson Monument

Main Street, Chatham, MA
- Distance: 330 feet
- Walking Time: 2 minutes

Directions:

Turn left out of the park, and continue down the north side of Main Street for another 300 feet. Look for the bronze marker set into stone monument.

Description:

William Nickerson arrived in the autumn of his life to Chatham. As a late comer (not having come over on the *Mayflower* or descended from one who had), he had no authority to purchase land from the local Monomoit tribe. But he did so in 1656, and it only took a dozen years to clear up the property title. In the mean time, he brought a large extended family to settle in Chathamport. The center of town took another hundred and fifty years to settle in this location.

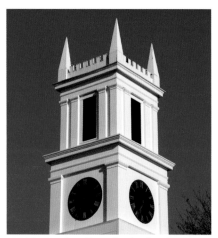

Methodist Church. *Author's photo.*

Josiah Mayo House. *Author's photo.*

Josiah Mayo House. *From a private collection.*

5) Eldredge Public Library
Main Street, Chatham, MA
www.eldredgelibrary.org
- Distance: 50 feet
- Walking Time: 1 minute

Directions:
The library is directly behind the Settlers Monument.

Description:
Marcellus Eldredge, who brought the railroad to Chatham, built and donated the original front section of the library in 1896. Upon entering, his portrait, set high above, greets you like the Gilded-Age patriarch he was. The reference room and fiction corners are good places to curl up undisturbed with a book, like a true Victorian.

6) Mayo House
540 Main Street, Chatham, MA
508-945-6098
www.chathamconservationfoundation.org
- Distance: 275 feet
- Walking Time: 1 minute

Directions:
From the front of the library, take a left and continue down the sidewalk. The Cape Cod Five will be on your left and the Town Offices on the right. The Mayo House is just after the bank, on your right.

Description:
Built in 1818 by Josiah Mayo, this little three-quarter Cape served as the post office, a dry good store, and later a repository of the town records. Recently, my family came across Josiah Mayo's family bible, and we donated it to the Chatham Conservation Foundation for use here. Open seasonally.

Kate Gould
Park.
*Author's
photo.*

Whit
Tileston
Bandstand.
*Author's
photo.*

Nautilus.
*Author's
photo.*

7) Kate Gould Park & Whit Tileston Bandstand
500 Main Street, Chatham, MA
- Distance: 400 feet
- Walking Time: 2 minutes

Directions:
As you leave the front of the Mayo House, take a left and continue down Main Street for another 400 feet. Look for the white fence entrance to the park on your left. Look for the stone marker straight ahead on the path.

Description:
If you're here any other time than Friday night in the summer, remember how peaceful and serene it was. Once a week, at the height of the season, 6,000 people will crowd into this small park and surround the bandstand to hear old-time favorites and dance the bunny hop. It's been going strong for over 70 years.

8) Nautilus
115 Main Street, Chatham, MA
- Distance: 0.8 miles
- Walking Time: 15 minutes

Directions:
From the bandstand, exit the park through the rear parking lot to Chatham Bars Ave. Cross the street to the brick building and take a right onto the sidewalk. Follow the sidewalk to the corner with Main Street, across from the Mayflower shop.

Cross Main Street and take a left onto the sidewalk. Follow this for another 0.4 miles. Here, the road will curve to right along a white picket fence, with Shore Road intersecting on the left.

Continue along the right hand side of Main Street, along the sidewalk, for almost another 0.3 miles, where Water Street crosses Main Street.

Description:
David Gould, Jr., built the original front of the house about 1838. In the 1920s it passed into the hands of the Barton family, and it became one of the many summer rooming houses down by the lighthouse, when lower Main Street was the commercial

Mack Memorial. *Author's photo.*

district. Dubbed *Nautilus*, no doubt because of its many rooms, it continued as such into the early 1980s.

In the summer of 1993, two friends and I stayed there to complete minor renovations, with evenings punctuated by sitting on the front porch and inviting any and all passers-by to join us in song and poetry. My subsequent novel, *The Bostoner*, was heavily influenced by my time there – and the eerie similarity in the design of *Nautilus* with that of the Captain John Kendrick House in Wareham, down to identical furniture.

While there, we were told by people who had summered there earlier that the place was definitely haunted. The story when that a sea captain had come home early from a voyage and found his wife in bed with another man. He promptly killed both, then himself. Well, the fact is, David Gould, Jr, was killed instantly when a load of rope fell on him in 1889, so we're not sure where the ghost story came from. But we all experienced the creeps there, especially with the beam of the lighthouse flashing in our windows every few seconds in the dark of night.

The Bartons sold the place at the turn of the millennium and it has obviously been completely renovated. No word yet on paranormal activity.

9) Mack Memorial
    61 Main Street, Chatham, MA
    • Distance: 500 feet
    • Walking Time: 2 minutes

Directions:
    Continue along Main Street for another 500 feet. Look on your right for a tall granite obelisk, across from the ocean overlook and parking. Walk up the steps.

Description:
    There is no better marker of the transition to the Outer Cape than right here. Up to this point, we've been looking inward, at the homes and lives of those who made their fortunes in the interior. This monument tells a different tale. When you faced the open Atlantic, often times it meant hardship. Seven men from the life saving station lost their lives attempting to save the owner, captain, and crew of the stranded coal barge *Wadena*. Only one of the rescuers survived, who was subsequently recovered through the heroics of Captain Elmer Mayo of Chatham.

Battle of Chatham Harbor Monument. *Author's photo.*

Lighthouse Beach. *Author's photo.*

Pendleton Monument. *Author's photo.*

CG36500 Motor Life Boat rescue by Richard Kaiser. *Courtesy of U.S. Coast Guard.*

10) Battle of Chatham Harbor

60 Main Street, Chatham, MA
- Distance: 120 feet
- Walking Time: 1 minutes

Directions:
From the memorial, cross Main Street. Look for the marker at the extreme left (north) end of the parking lot.

Description:
With the commencement of war, Chatham fishermen and sailors were put at risk by British warships and privateers. The abundant fishing industry as virtually closed. Chatham men responded by becoming privateers themselves, preying on English shipping on both sides of the Atlantic, or joining the militia. Captain Benjamin Godfrey, whose company of minutemen drove off the British raider in Chatham Harbor, also served at Bunker Hill.

11) Pendleton Monument

38 Main Street, Chatham, MA
www.cg36500.org
- Distance: 400 feet
- Walking Time: 2 minutes

Directions:
From the battle marker, walk down the parking lot, keeping the ocean on your left. The monument is a stone marker on your left, before the stairs.

Description:
Twenty-five years after the tanker *Pendleton* went down, I recall going out to the wreck (one mile east of Monomoy Island, 6 miles down the shore to the right) in a small skiff. The dark hull of the ship stuck straight up out of the water, covered with a bright red coat of rust... and a brighter white coating, evidence of dozens years of seagull presence. A year later, the "Blizzard of '78" destroyed most of what lay above the water line, and the Coast Guard demolished what was left as a hazard to navigation. Divers still go out the site, mostly to hunt lobsters.

Chatham Lighthouse & U.S. Coast Guard Station. *Author's photo.*

When they were teenagers, my sisters used to gather up their kid brother and head off to Lighthouse Beach for the day – the whole day – with nothing but diet iced tea, tuna fish sandwiches, and light rock playing on the AM radio.

At the time, a barrier beach protected the whole of Chatham Harbor. In 1987, a nor'easter punched a hole in the beach, creating North Beach on your left and South Beach on your right. South Beach connected to the mainland in 1991, and then another nor'easter rammed across North Beach further up in 2007. Beaches become islands and islands attach themselves somewhere else. The only things that haven't changed are that the three binoculars overlooking the break are still a quarter – and that in the summer, guys still take their lunch break up here to check out the bikinis below.

12) Chatham Lighthouse & U.S. Coast Guard Station
37 Main Street, Chatham, MA
508 430-0628
www.uscg.mil/d1/Units/gruwh/stachatham
• Distance: 275 feet
• Walking Time: 1 minutes

Directions:
From the stairs, cross the street to the fence in front of the lighthouse.

Description:
There's been a lighthouse at Chatham since 1808, with the town hosting three lighthouses up until the 1950s — at Chatham Harbor, Stage Harbor, and Monomoy Point. Chatham Light was originally twin lights, replaced more than once. But in 1923 the north tower was moved to Eastham to become the new Nauset Light. In 1969 the light in the south tower was replaced with a high-intensity beacon. Lighthouse tours are given Wednesdays from May through October.

Monomoy National Wildlife Refuge (NWR) entrance. *Author's photo.*

Visitor's Center, Monomoy NWR. *Author's photo.*

13) Monomoy National Wildlife Refuge
30 Wikis Way, Chatham, MA 02633
508 945-0594
monomoy.fws.gov
- Distance: 1.4 miles
- Driving Time: 5 minutes

Directions:
If you are biking, continue with this stop. If you're walking, consider hitting this at the end of the trip, once you get back in your car. Skip the rest of the directions here and go to the directions for the Mitchell Rive Bridge.

Biking: Follow Main Street as it passes the tennis courts on your left, and ends at intersection with Silverleaf Ave and Bridge Street. Bear to the left and continue down the hill on Morris Island Road.

Follow it for 0.2 miles, then turn right to continue on Morris Island Road. If you miss this and go straight, you'll end up at Outermost marine.

Continue on Morris Island Road for another ¾ miles. At the end of the Morris Island dike, you will see a sign on your left for the Monomoy National Wildlife Refuge. Continue up the hill, ignoring the signs saying "Residents Only" (the federal government is the largest resident in the neighborhood), and take your first left onto Wiki's Way. At the parking lot, bear right and head to the Refuge headquarters in the rear. Once you've covered the whole area here, retrace your route back to the intersection with Bridge Street and Main Street.

Description:
Monomoy is the recipient of half the erosion of the Outer Cape (the other half going to Provincetown, at the other end of the Great Beach), and has been at times connected to the mainland, then an island, then two islands, and, at present, partially connected again. I try to every year walk down the end of South Beach from in front of the Chatham Lighthouse, taking usually two and a half hours of trudging in sand, one way. In December 2006, I walked the distance to the new connection to the northern tip of South Monomoy Island — a place that, during my life, had only been accessible by boat. As both a wilderness and wildlife refuge, not being an island anymore presents certain challenges.

Overlooking the Southway and South Beach, Monomoy NWR.
Author's photo.

Weather balloon
release station,
Monomoy NWR.
Author's photo.

Mitchell River Bridge. *Author's photo.*

The broad flats of Monomoy, next to the cool waters of the open Atlantic, are ideal for shellfish. Having spent many years as a commercial clamdigger there, I was often accompanied by kindred spirits — chiefly, shorebirds. That's what Monomoy NWR is really about — especially protecting those plovers that President Grover Cleveland was so fond of blasting away at (mentioned in the previous Tour of the Canal area).

Looking out across the Southway, beyond South Beach, you may see some breakers and shoals in the ocean. Those sand bars and rips are what the Mayflower encountered in the winter of 1620. Heading towards the Hudson River and New Amsterdam, they were 200 miles off-course and could not get around this rough patch of water. So they instead turned north, eventually settling in Plymouth. As a descendant, I have to wonder. If not for those breakers, would I have grown up in patrician comfort amongst Roosevelts and Vanderbilts?

When weather radar first came in common use, I recall the watching the Boston broadcasts and seeing the center of the map being in Chatham. Technology marched on, and newer, more powerful station off-Cape took over the job. But being so close to the Gulf Stream, weather balloons are still released twice daily from the building here.

14) Mitchell River Bridge
Bridge Street, Chatham, MA
508-945-5185
• Distance: 0.6 miles
• Walking Time: 15 minutes

Directions:
Follow Main Street as it passes the tennis courts on your left, and ends at intersection with Silverleaf Ave and Bridge Street. Bear right onto Bridge Street and continue for half a mile to the bridge. If you're driving, limited parking is beyond the bridge and off to the right.

Description:
The original drawbridge was built in 1854, and allows for the many larger sailboats to get up from Stage Harbor up into Pease Boatworks on the Mill Pond. It is also a popular spot for fishing with just a drop line baited with a few green mussels gathered from along the shore.

The Atwood House. *Author's photo.*

Joseph Atwood House, 1935, photographed by Arthur C. Haskell. *Courtesy of Historic American Buildings Survey.*

Nickerson North Beach Camp. *Author's photo.*

15) The Atwood House Museum
347 Stage Harbor Road, Chatham, MA
www.chathamhistoricalsociety.org
508 945-2493
- Distance: 0.6 miles
- Driving Time: 15 minutes

Directions:
Continue on Bridge Street for 0.2 miles. At the T-intersection with Stage Harbor Road, turn right and head up the hill. The Atwood House is 1/3 of a mile up on your right.

Description:
This is the oldest house in Chatham. While the grounds around the place that Joseph Atwood built during the French and Indian War have changed greatly, the main house certainly hasn't. Inside you'll find an efficiency of space above all else. But when you live at the end of a treeless peninsula known for clammy, windy winters (or, for that matter, clammy, windy summers), you won't be wasteful with your framing timbers or firewood.

Inside the museum, make sure to check out the exhibit in the fishing gallery. Outside, you'll see the old Fresnel lens removed from the top of Chatham light in 1969, and the Nickerson North Beach camp, rescued from certain destruction on North Beach.

Former Chatham Light lantern house. *Author's photo*

Doc Keene Scout Hall. *Author's photo.*

Chase Park. *Author's photo.*

16) Doc Keene Scout Hall
224 Stage Harbor Road, Chatham, MA
• Distance: 0.25 miles
• Walking Time: 8 minutes

Directions:
Leaving the Atwood House, take a right onto Stage Harbor Road. The Scout Hall is on the left side, at the intersection with Cedar Street.

Description:
Not exactly a one-room schoolhouse (it has two floors), the Atwood School was one of many neighborhood schools around Chatham. Built in 1869, it continued use as a primary school until the consolidation of all schools in 1926. At that time, Doc Keene started the local chapter of the Boy Scouts. When I attended meetings there in the 1970s, it was already in poor shape. In the 1990s volunteers began renovations. Only another dozen years and $175,000 in town funding were needed to finish the job, showing that, although the glacier retreated 10,000 years ago, some local pockets remain.

17) Chase Park
101 Cross Street, Chatham, MA
508 945-5175
• Distance: 0.3 miles
• Walking Time: 10 minutes

Directions:
From the Scout Hall, cross Cedar Street, then cross Stage Harbor Road to the mouth of Cross Street. Follow the sidewalk on the left side of Cross Street for 0.2 miles. The entrance to the park is on the right, opposite Henshaw Drive.

Description:
Except for the Creative Arts Festival in mid-August, Chase Park remains otherwise peaceful throughout the year. Although a popular place for dog-walkers, owners are extremely good about cleaning up. There are even picnic tables and barbecue grills here. Because of its proximity to downtown, this is a regular stop on Sunday mornings for my daughter and me to take our doughnuts.

Godfrey Windmill. *Author's photo.*

Godfrey Windmill in its original location on Mill Hill, overlooking Stage Harbor. *From a private collection.*

Chatham Bars Inn overlooking Shore Road and Chatham Harbor. *Author's photo*

18) Godfrey Windmill
Shattuck Place, Chatham, MA
- Distance: 950 feet
- Walking Time: 5 minutes

Directions:
At the far end of Chase Park, cross the parking lot and continue up the hill to Windmill.

Description:
Colonel Benjamin Godfrey, who chased away the British from Chatham Harbor, built this mill in 1797. It sat atop aptly-named Mill Hill, between the Mitchell River Bridge and the Atwood House, and continued grinding corn for 100 years. It was given to the town in 1956 and moved here. The mill has intermittent hours through the summer.

19) Chatham Bars Inn
297 Shore Road, Chatham, MA 02633
508 945-0096
www.chathambarsinn.com
- Distance: 0.9 miles
- Walking Time: 20 minutes

Directions:
From the Windmill, turn right onto Shattuck Place and follow down the intersection with Cross Street. Turn right onto the sidewalk opposite, and follow Cross Street down to Main Street.

At the Methodist Church, turn left onto Main Street, then cross onto the left (north) hand side. Turn left, and follow to the intersection with Seaview Street and Sears Park. Keep the park on your left and continue up Seaview on the sidewalk. On this side, the sidewalk ends, so cross over to the left hand side. Follow Seaview Street for another third of a mile, past the golf course. Turn right onto Kettle Drum Lane, then take your first left into the rear entrance of Chatham Bars Inn, and pass through the lobby.

Chatham Bars Inn stretching northward to the Fish Pier.
Courtesy of capecardart.com.

Description:

When Marcellus Eldredge brought the railroad, he keenly built the Hotel Chatham in Chathamport — a massive shingle-style concern with broad porches and a commanding view. However, it never prospered and within 20 years it was broken apart for smaller uses. Many of the finer bones salvaged made their way into the Chatham Bars Inn when it was built in 1914.

Although much of the Cape is sandy soil, parts are fairly fertile. Chatham Bars Inn provisioned itself through its own farm on the north side of the Oyster Pond, outside town. Growing up there and in charge of the lawn mower, I can attest that the grass grows faster there than anywhere on earth. And, just last year, 50 years after the farm closed, my daughter found an intact glass milk bottle in the meadowbank of the pond, reading "Chatham Bars Inn Farm."

Chatham Bars Inn from across Shore Road. *Author's photo.*

Chatham Fish Pier and Nickerson's Fish & Lobsters. *Author's photo.*

Awaiting the next unloading of fish, Chatham Fish Pier. *Author's photo.*

Fish Pier and boats. *Author's photo.*

Viewing platform, Chatham Fish Pier. *Author's photo.*

20) Chatham Municipal Fish Pier

54 Barcliff Avenue Extension, Chatham, MA
508-945-5177
• Distance: 0.25 miles
• Walking Time: 8 minutes

Directions:

From the front of CBI, cross Shore Road and take a left. Continue along the brick sidewalk for 0.2 miles, until you come to the Fish Pier parking lot. Turn right and go down the stairs past the Fishermen's monument. Follow the crosswalk to past Nickerson's fish market to the stairs to the Fish Pier.

Description:

Being so much closer to the open ocean, Chatham fishermen operate a day-fishery, meaning they don't need to spend a day or more just getting to their grounds. Also, the shallowness of the harbor doesn't lend itself to larger boats. Aunt Lydia's Cove, offers a fair amount of protection from storms for the largest commercial fishing fleet on Cape Cod. Anytime a hurricane passes within 500 miles, watch for local and national weathercasters to report from either this spot or the Lighthouse. They usually spend about five seconds in front of the camera, attempting to look like a piece of the scenery before retreating to the safety of their comfy broadcast vans.

From the viewing platform, you not only can watch the comings and going of the fleet, but from directly overhead, the unloading of fish direct from the shore to the packing house. A stray seal or two are also likely to pop up their head. Gulls, as always around Chatham, are ubiquitous.

Wrapping it Up: Further directions

• Distance: 0.8 miles
• Walking Time: 20 minutes

The driveway that leads down the hill to the Fish Pier the end of Barcliff Ave Extension. Follow the road back up the hill to the stop sign. Cross Shore Road, past the home of the late Senator Paul Tsongas and U.S. Rep. Niki Tsongas on the far right corner. Continue on Barcliff Ave for 0.3 mile until you come to Old Harbor Road.

Bikers: If you wish to return to the bike trail, continue straight on Barcliff and it will bring you back to where you started.

Walkers: Take a left onto Old Harbor Road and continue for 0.4 mile to Depot Road. Cross Old Harbor Road to Depot to the sidewalk on the left hand side. The Railroad Museum is 500 feet up on your right.

Orleans. *Courtesy of Cape Cod Aerial Photography.*

Graveyard of the Atlantic

The Outer Cape:

Orleans, Eastham & Wellfleet

"Everything indicated that we had reached a strange shore." *Henry David Thoreau*, Cape Cod

Overall Distance: 23.5 miles
Time: 5 hours
Public Restrooms: Orleans downtown: Snow Library, Orleans Town Hall; Eastham Information Booth; Eastham Library; Eastham Town Hall; Salt Pond Visitors Center; Nauset Coast Guard Station; Marconi Station; Wellfleet Information Booth; Wellfleet Town Hall

Note: Giles Hopkins, who came over on the *Mayflower* as a young teenager with his family, first moved to Yarmouth soon after it was founded in 1639, then moved again in 1650 to the head of Town Cove in Orleans.

My mother, Lucy Jane Buckley, was born a Hopkins in Eastham. She grew during the Depression up on a farm on Hopkins Lane in East Orleans. When her youngest son was born, he was given the middle name of Giles, hearkening back ten generations. I always like my middle name, and believe that everyone should have a cool story about theirs.

So, other than the fact that I come from a family that came across the ocean, took a sharp left, went 50 miles and stayed put for 400 years, what good is it? Well, it never got me into an Ivy League school or a seat on the New York Stock Exchange. But when it comes to my ancestral lands, I know my way around.

Old King's Highway marker, Brewster-
Orleans line. *Author's photo.*

Rock Harbor. *Author's photo.*

The restored CG36500 Motor LIfe Boat. *Courtesy of Nicholas Leach.*

1) CG36500 Life Boat,

Rock Harbor Road, & Bay View Drive,
Orleans, MA
508-240-1329
www.cg36500.org

If you hold up your arm to represent Cape Cod, Rock Harbor is at the very inside of your elbow, on Cape Cod Bay.

Founded in 1787, Orleans is the hub of the Lower/Outer Cape, with plenty of places to grab a bite to eat. With its northern neighbors, Eastham, Wellfleet, and Truro, formed the town of Nauset, founded by the Pilgrims in 1644. We'll be doing a lot of criss-crossing of their old stomping grounds on this tour, so make sure you pick up a few supplies, meaning food, drink, and, in season, maybe sunblock and bug spray. Traffic can get kind of hairy in the summer, and doubly so if it isn't a sunny "beach day" — everyone will be on the roads. Once out of the center of town, there won't be much chance for picking up anything… without having to retrace your steps on roads that you do not want to turn around on.

Directions:

Wherever you're coming from, find your way to the center of Orleans — meaning, the stop lights at the intersection of Main Street and Route 6A. Get on Main Street heading northwest keeping the small cemetery on your left. Head out of town over the bike trail and past Snow's Hardware on your right. Main Street soon becomes Rock Harbor Road, and will practically dead-end at the harbor after a couple minutes. Take a left into the parking lot (a/k/a Bay View Drive) and drive all the way down to the end. CG36500 is berthed on the dock along your right.

Description:

When she's not out participating in one event or the other, CG36500, of Pendleton fame (see tour of Chatham) is berthed here. Decommissioned in 1968, the volunteers rescued the rescue boat in 1981. The Orleans Historical Society now maintains it as floating museum.

As you look out the harbor, you'll see the trees marking the entrance to the deep but narrow channel. When I was a kid, you could very clearly watch the sun set through the remains of a Liberty Ship, the USS James Longstreet, which had been sunk Cape Cod Bay and used for target practice by the Navy. If you're interested in going out fishing, inquire with one of the many charter boats at Rock Harbor.

Civil War Monument. *Courtesy of capecardart.com.*

Orleans Historical Society Museum. *Author's photo.*

2) Orleans Historical Society Meeting House Museum

3 River Road, Orleans, MA 02653

508-240-1329

orleanshistoricalsociety.org

• Distance: 2.1 miles
• Driving Time: 8 minutes

Directions:

From Rock Harbor, proceed out of the parking lot and take a right onto Rock Harbor Road. After a mile, Rock Harbor Road changes its name and becomes Main Street. Drive for another mile, going through two stop lights (the first crossing Route 6A and the second crossing Route 28), and passing the Civil War Monument on your right.

The Museum is on the right hand side, across from the Orleans Cemetery. Take a right into the parking lot just before River Road.

If you pass the cemetery and see the Federated Church with the onion dome, turn around and take an immediate left onto School Road. The Orleans Town Hall on your left, just past the intersection with River Road. The Museum is directly across the street.

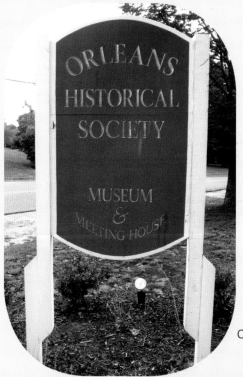

Orleans HSM

Reuben S.B. Hopkins. *Courtesy of the Hopkins Family collection.*

Description:

In the summer of 1918, a German U-boat was cruising along the outer shore of Cape Cod, looking to cut the Transatlantic telegraph cable to the Allies in Europe and otherwise menace shipping. It surfaced off the Orleans Life Saving Station and started firing upon a barge making its way along the coast. While the men of the station made their way out to rescue the crew of the tug, a signalman was left behind to relay direction from the watchtower.

Eventually, flying boats from Naval Air Station Chatham made their way here. But what torpedoes were dropped were duds. In frustration, one of the pilots grabbed the only means he had at hand, a monkey wrench, and threw it at the submarine. Having done its damage, the U-boat disappeared — then resurfaced directly in front of the station, and fired at the tower. The signalman reported that it sounded like a train coming through a tunnel as the shell passed by his head. At least, that's the way the story was told to me as a kid by my brother.

This was the only time since the War of 1812 that enemy fire landed on the mainland of the United States. And that man in the tower was my grandfather, Reuben Hopkins. He was also a founding member of the Orleans Historical Society. Their Meeting House Museum is open from June to September one limited hours. Call ahead to view exhibits on the U-Boat attack and other memorable parts of Orleans history.

Rescued crew hauled to shore. *Courtesy of the Hopkins Family collection.*

French Transatlantic Cable
Station Museum.
Author's photo.

3) French Transatlantic Cable Station Museum

41 South Orleans Road, Orleans, MA

508 240-1735

www.atlantic-cable.com

- Distance: 0.8 miles
- Driving Time: 3 minutes

Directions:

From the parking lot across from the Orleans Cemetery, take a left onto Main Street. Drive for half a mile on Main Street (again passing the Civil War Monument). After the first set of stop lights, notice the area to your right as it opens up at the head of Town Cove. This is where Giles Hopkins settled down in 1650.

When you can see the next stop light, at the intersection with Route 28, bear right onto Academy Place. Drive about 450 feet to the stop sign, and bear right onto Route 28.

After another 400 feet, the French Cable Museum will be on your right. Turn right onto Cove Road and park in the immediate rear.

Description:

This is where the Germans were headed — well, not exactly. The French laid the first Transatlantic cable, from Brest to Newfoundland and Duxbury (near Plymouth) in 1869 — previously all communication had to be physically by carried 3,000 miles by ship. A second cable was laid in 1879, this one terminating in North Eastham, next to Nauset Light.

The story goes that the cable operators, who were set up with their families out there, apparently were not artistic-types who thrived on isolation. So this station was built in the heart of Orleans, with a cable running through Town Cove and across Nauset marsh to what became known as the French Cable Hut. This was one of only five cables to Europe during World War I, so it would have been a major disruption if the Germans had been able to cut it. But submarines don't work so well in broad areas of turbulent, shallow water.

Jonathan Young Windmill, Orleans. *Author's photo.*

4) Jonathan Young Windmill

Route 6A at Town Cove, Orleans, MA
508-240-1329
- Distance: 0.6 miles
- Driving Time: 5 minutes

Directions:

Take a left onto Cove Road, and then an immediate right onto Route 28.

After 0.3 miles Route 28 will merge into Route 6. There are two lanes created for northbound traffic, one dedicated to traffic coming from Route 28 (like you), so there is no need for a stop or yield sign. If you feel you must stop here anyway, you run a greater risk of being rear-ended. But stay in the right hand lane.

In another 0.3 miles, you will see the windmill and Town Cove on your right. There is stop light just after.

At the light, take a hairpin right into what appears to be the parking lot of the Orleans Inn. Head down the gravel driveway toward the windmill's parking.

Description:

Like Chatham's, this windmill got around. Built about 1720 in South Orleans, it was moved in 1839 on the hill you just passed by. Then, sixty years later, it went to live at a private home in Hyannisport. Finally, it was offered to the Orleans Historical Society 25 years ago, and ended up here in a new park. It is very well maintained, using much of its original machinery.

Old King's
Highway marker:
Orleans-Eastham
line. *Author's
photo.*

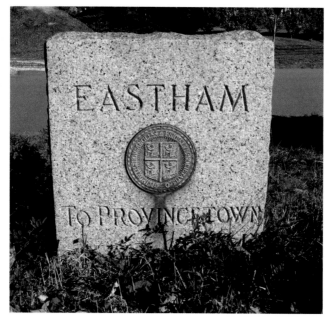

Old King's
Highway marker:
Eastham-Orleans
line. *Author's
photo.*

5) Cove Burying Ground

Opposite the junction of Route 6 & Hay Road, Eastham, MA

508 240-5900

www.eastham-ma.gov

• Distance: 1.5 miles
• Driving Time: 5 minutes

Directions:

Leaving the parking lot, do not attempt to take a left and wait for the stop light. Instead, proceed straight, past the Orleans Inn on your right, along Old County Road.

Drive almost 400 feet, past the marina and Ellis Road, and take the first left. This is a short paved road will bring you back to Route 6A.

At the stop sign, take a right onto Route 6A and stay right.

Almost immediately, the two lanes heading northbound merge into one — you will now enter the Orleans Rotary.

Note on the Rotary: If you have little experience with a rotary, just remember that in Massachusetts, traffic entering must yield to traffic already in the rotary. So as you enter the rotary, watch out for high-speed traffic coming from your extreme left. These are cars coming from the Mid-Cape Highway (Route 6). But you should not come to a complete stop or you will risk a rear-end collision. Merge.

You, too, are heading north on Route 6, and so stick to the right hand side, and you and your zooming neighbors will enter the two northbound lanes of Route 6 side-by-side, into Eastham.

If you somehow get sucked into the Rotary, go around it entirely. Do not take the first exit — you will eventually end up back at Rock Harbor. Do not take the second — you be taken westbound on Route 6 and eventually off-Cape. Do not take the third exit — you will head back towards the windmill, with little chance to turn around. Just hang on and remember that in the rotary (in theory) you have the right-of-way.

After the rotary, stay in the right lane. After a mile, look for Hay Road on your left. Across the street will be a small paved and dirt pull-off with the sign "Cove Burying Ground" in front of the cemetery. Take a sharp right and park on the gravel and sand.

Description:

There's usually a handout here, so I'll try not to repeat what it says. Pretty much, in New England, when you find the oldest cemetery in town, that's where the meeting house (church/town hall/school combined) was — so this was the original center of town. Might not look like much now, with the cars speeding behind you and crowded in by the red cedars. But at the time, it overlooked the mouth of Town Cove, where it flows into Nauset Harbor.

The first stone you'll notice on your left is that of Constance Hopkins Snow. Her younger brother, Giles, has a marker up on the left. But we know about him already. It's his mother-in-law who is interesting. The story goes that in 1608, a group of Wampanoags were picked up by an English ship off Cape Cod, including a six year old girl named Oguina. They were taken back to London, where she was Anglicized and became Margaret Wampanoag, later marrying Gabriel Wheldon. Whether this was a first or second marriage, and whether there were step-children or they had kids together is not clear. But what is known is that Gabriel and Margaret Wheldon came to Plymouth, and his daughter, Catherine, married Giles Hopkins.

Which, compared with Austin Bearse of Barnstable (see the Route 6A tour), turns on its head the idea of moving to a new place and marrying one of the locals. It also blurs the concept of the separateness of settlers and natives, which is probably a good thing. Then and now.

Opposite, top; Cove Burying Ground.
Bottom; Angel of Death,
Cove Burying Ground.
Author's photo

Fort Hill from the trail. *Courtesy of capecardart.com.*

Samuel De Champlain by Louis-César-Joseph Ducornet. *Courtesy of Library and Archives Canada.*

Red Maple Swamp Trail. *Courtesy of capecardart.com.*

6) Fort Hill

200 Fort Hill Road, Eastham, MA
• Distance: 0.8 miles
• Driving Time: 3 minutes

Directions:

Proceed 200 feet along the small paved road parallel to Route 6 until you come to Corliss Way, on your right. Take it and turn right onto Route 6. After 0.3 mile, bear right onto Governor Prence at the sign saying "Fort Hill Area." After 0.2 mile, the Governor Prence forks — take a right up the hill and bear right onto Fort Hill Road. Drive another 0.3 miles, past an ornate yellow house on your right, and up the hill until you reach the parking lot at the end. If available, park on the left for the best view.

Description:

Like many villages of the natives, there was the place you camped out for the summer, close to food and other resources, and the place you retreated to in the winter, for shelter. The "fort" referred to in the name was actually the summer village of the Nauset, and its easy to see why they chose it. Likewise, you can see why the Pilgrims chose to set up shop close by.

Samuel de Champlain cruised through here in 1605, and later wrote of the Nausets, "They are not so much great hunters as good fishermen and tillers of the land." Fort Hill holds some of the most fertile land on the otherwise sandy Outer Cape.

As you look out across the water, to the sea, follow the beach to the left and you'll notice the tall white building on a bluff. That is the old Estham Coast Guard Station and we'll be headed there after a few more stops.

Approaching Nauset Marsh at the bottom of Fort Hill. *Courtesy of capecardart. com.*

Looking across Nauset Marsh from Fort Hill.
Author's photo.

7) Captain Penniman House
70 Fort Hill Road, Eastham, MA
- Distance: 0.5 miles
- Walking Time: 10 minutes

Directions:
There are a few options here. You can walk the trail to Sharpening Rock, and after reaching the lower parking lot, cross the street to the Penniman House. Depending upon your walking speed, that could take the better part of an hour.

Or you could take the waterside trail that hooks around to the south of Fort Hill and come up behind the Penniman House. That could take 5-10 minutes.

Or you could drive down the hill to the lower parking area, and walk across to the Penniman House. It will take longer to get in and out of your car than to drive it.

Description:
Yes, those are the jawbones of a whale framing the entrance. Edward Penniman built this house with the proceeds from his fourth whaling voyage. Since those could take up to four years a piece, he obviously wanted to live in some style and comfort. It was the first house in town to have indoor plumbing, after all.

Captain Edward Penniman House. Author's photo.

8) Old Eastham Windmill
Route 6 and Samoset Road, Eastham, MA
508 240-5900
www.eastham-ma.gov
• Distance: 1 mile driving, +500 feet walking
• Walking Time: 10 minutes

Directions:
From either parking lot, get back on Fort Hill Road passing the Penniman House on your left. Returning to the split with Governor Prence Road on your left, continue straight. When you reach the stop sign at Route 6, take a right. Stay in the right lane. **NOTE:** On entering Route 6, the Eastham Information Booth will be on your immediate right.

Drive on Route 6 for 0.8 mile. Just before the stop light, take a right into the Town Hall Parking Lot. Find a parking spot close to the stop light. From your car, walk along the sidewalk directly in front of Town Hall. The crosswalk in front of the stoplight has a walk signal (and it actually works). Cross Route 6 and enter the Windmill Park.

Description:
The granddaddy (or grandmommy) of them all, this is the oldest on the Cape, built in 1680 — in Plymouth. And, of course, it traveled, first to Truro in 1770, and then to the hill above the Mill Pond in 1793. It's only been in this spot across from Town Hall for a mere 200 years. Plus, it works! The miller is there most days July and August.

Old Eastham Windmill. *Courtesy of capecardart.com.*

The Swift-Daley House. *Courtesy of capecardart.com.*

The Swift-Daley House. *Author's photo.*

9)The Swift-Daley House
Route 6, Eastham, MA
508 240-1247
www.easthamhistorical.org
• Distance: 1,000 feet
• Driving Time: 7 minutes

Directions:
From the windmill and facing Route 6, take a right and out the south exit. Cross Samoset Road, cross the parking lot, and follow the sidewalk south. The driveway to the Swift-Daley House is a few hundred feet down on the right. If you see the Eastham Post Office, you've gone too far.

Description:
My great-grandmother, Flora Knowles, lived not too far from here, in an unassuming cottage. I mention that because the Swift-Daley house was built by Joshua Knowles in 1741. The Daleys, who had bought the house in the 1930s and restored it, donated the house to the Eastham Historical Society in 1974, the year before "Nana" died at 93.

So keep three things in mind as you look about this bow-roofed house, with its big old hearth, nearly suicidal stairs and wide-board floors: first, this place was already an old house the day my great-grandmother was born, second, it looked that way the day she died, and lastly, it will remain in that condition far into the future.

Hands-on exhibits, Salt Pond Visitors Center. *Author's photo.*

Hay Barge, Salt Pond Visitors Center. *Author's photo.*

10) Salt Pond Visitor Center
50 Doane Rd, Eastham, MA 02642
508 255-3421
www.nps.gov/caco/planyourvisit/visitorcenters.htm
• Distance: 1 mile
• Walking/Driving Time: 8 minutes

Directions:
Exit Swift-Daley driveway as you came in, and return to your car via the sidewalk and the cross walk in front of Town Hall.

From Eastham Town Hall, turn onto Route 6 (right turn only). Through the stop light, stay in the right lane, keeping the fire and police stations on your right.

Drive half a mile and look for the sign for the Salt Pond Visitors Center. Bear right onto the exit, onto Nauset Road. Take the first driveway into the parking lot.

Restroom: Adjacent to the parking lot, to the left of the visitor center, with additional restrooms inside the visitors center.

Description:
Before you even look at anything else in here, you should know this was where the Eastham windmill used to be until 1808.

That said, you could spend a lot of time in here. To your right are exhibits on earlier life on the Outer Cape. To the left is the theater, which plays continuous documentaries on history and culture. And out back is a hay barge, a kind of boat designed to harvest the salt hay on the Nauset Marsh for cattle feed. This one had been used to maintain the cable leading from Eastham to the French cable station in Orleans — but probably was not equipped to defend against submarines.

Salt Pond Visitors Center, Cape Cod National Seashore. *Courtesy of capecardart.com.*

Eastham Schoolhouse Museum. *Courtesy of capecardart.com.*

Old King's Highway marker: Eastham Schoolhouse. *Author's photo.*

11) Schoolhouse Museum
Nauset and Schoolhouse Roads, Eastham, MA
508 240-1247
www.easthamhistorical.org
• Distance: 750 feet
• Walking/Driving Time: 5 minutes

Directions:
The passage through the parking lot and across the street to the Schoolhouse Museum is, by the wisdom of federal park officials of 50 years ago, not pedestrian friendly. But, depending upon where you parked in the visitor center lot, it may be as long a walk back to your car.

Walking: head out of the visitor's center and take a left at the foot of the walkway. Go out the driveway you came in on, cross the Nauset Road, and turn left onto Schoolhouse Road. Take your first left into the Schoohouse driveway.

Driving: Follow the parking lot to the exit and turn left onto Nauset Road. Follow Nauset Road, keeping the visitor's center on your left. Take a right onto Schoolhouse Road, across from the entrance to the visitor's center. Then take a left into the driveway.

Description:
Originally a one-room schoolhouse built in 1869, the North Eastham school was moved here and attached in 1908. A year later, the South Elementary School, which had been next to the Cove Burying Ground, was added on. It stopped being a school in the 1930s, and in 1967 was made into a museum by the Eastham Historical Society. They've just completed a major renovation in 2007, to provide greater space for exhibits. Outside, the grounds are scattered with memorials to those townsfolk who died in the service of their country.

12) Doane Rock

Doane Road & Tomahawk Trail, Eastham, MA
- Distance: 1 mile
- Driving Time: 4 minutes

Directions:

Take a left back onto Nauset Road, and keep the Visitor's Center on your right. After 0.6 miles, Nauset Road takes a left — but you should continue straight on Doane Road (you may not even see the change) for another 0.3 miles. Look for the sign for Doane Rock, and take a right onto Tomahawk Trail. Take your first left into the parking lot and find the first space you can.

Description:

This big rock appeared even bigger a hundred or more years ago, when all the trees had been chopped down. It's 18 feet above the ground and 12 feet below it. The glacier that made the Cape 18,000 years ago pretty much scraped the top off of Maine, ground it up and dumped it offshore. And to carry a stone this big, that glacier would have to have been one to two miles thick. As that ice melted, it flooded all of Nantucket Sound and Cape Cod Bay.

Doane Rock. *Courtesy of capecardart.com.*

13) Old Eastham Coast Guard Station
1 Ocean View Drive, Eastham, MA
- Distance: 0.6 miles (walking)
  /0.9 miles (driving)
- Walking/Driving Time: 15 minutes (walking)/
  3 minutes (driving)

Directions:
During the summer, the parking lots at Coast Guard Beach, adjacent to the Station, and Nauset Light Beach, are closed to all but Eastham residents. Instead, the National Park Service operates shuttles from satellite parking areas. One is located directly across Doane Road from Doane Rock. Otherwise, between Memorial Day and Labor Day, you can walk or bike the trail. It is gently rolling, ending with a boardwalk bridge across the marsh, coming up behind the Coast Guard Station. In the off-season, parking is not normally a problem.

Driving: From the parking lot, take a right onto Tomahawk Trail. At Doane Road, take a right and drive half a mile to the end. You should see the beach and ocean directly ahead, while the road appears to hook left. Take a right into the driveway for the Coast Guard Station, past the gate house and park at the top of the hill.

The Great Beach in winter. *Courtesy of capecardart.com.*

Eastham Coast
Guard Station.
Author's photo.

Coast Guard Beach. *Courtesy of capecardart.com*

Description:

You probably don't need to be told you are looking at the best beach on the East Coast (Lighthouse Beach in Chatham is second, due only to a lack of facilities and surf).

In 1924, Henry Beston spent a week in a 20' x 16' dune shack, dubbed "the Fo'castle," on the beach south of here. Then, as he wrote in *The Outermost House:*

> *The fortnight ending, I lingered on, and as the year lengthened into autumn, the beauty and mystery of this earth and outer sea so possessed and held me that I could not go.*

Like Thoreau, the botanist drawn to Walden Pond, Beston was an ornithologist drawn to the Great Beach. So I've been told he wasn't particularly fond of my grandfather and my great-uncles, who kept a duck blind between here and Fort Hill, on Nauset Marsh.

From time to time, Beston would trudge up the beach to Coast Guard Station, for coffee, doughnuts, and human contact. Likewise, the lifesavers, doing regular foot patrols of the beach, would stop into the Fo'castle to check on Beston and warm up.

After the Blizzard of '78, I remember coming down here with my father. There had been a large parking lot behind the beach, but the storm — a winter hurricane — had washed it and the Outermost House away.

Nauset Light. *Author's photo.*

The Three Sisters Lighthouses. *Courtesy of capecardart.com.*

14) Nauset Light

Nauset Light Beach Road, Eastham, MA
508 240-2612
www.nausetlight.org
- Distance: 1 mile
- Driving Time: 4 minutes

Directions:

If you took the shuttle or walked here from Doane Rock, wait for another take you to Nauset Light — unless you want to hike a mile up the beach.

NOTE: If you walked here from Doane Rock in the off-season, you'll have to walk back to your car — shuttles are summer-only.

Otherwise, follow the driveway back to the entrance. Bear right onto Ocean View Drive. Follow this for one mile until you reach a stop sign, with Cable Road on your left. You should see the white and red Nauset Light ahead.

Go through the stop sign — the road becomes Nauset Light Road — and take a sharp right into the parking lot.

Description:

Now, if you already did the Chatham Tour, this tower should look a little familiar. Until 1923, Chatham had twin lights. Then the north light was moved here and, in the 1940s, given a scarlet collar to differentiate it from her stay-at-home sister. They've had to keep moving the light back from the eroding cliff, too, the last time in 1996. The first lights here, "The Three Sisters" built in 1838, were located at top of the same cliff — but that was when the cliff was 800 feet further east.

You may recall that it was next to Nauset Light that the French Cable Hut was located — the original American terminus that was later extended to Orleans. The hut, along with the "Three Sisters", are located just off Nauset Light Road on the way to our next stop.

Here in Wellfleet... the solitude was that of the ocean and the desert combined. A thousand men could not have seriously interrupted it, but would have been lost in the vastness of the scenery as their footsteps in the sand.
— Henry David Thoreau, *Cape Cod.*

Old King's Highway marker: Wellfleet-Eastham line. *Author's photo.*

Marconi Station. *Author's photo.*

15) Marconi Station
End of Marconi Station Road, Wellfleet, MA
- Distance: 6 miles
- Driving Time: 15 minutes

Directions:
Exit the parking lot, taking a left onto Nauset Light Road. Bear right onto Cable Road and remember to watch for the Three Sisters lighthouses and the French Cable Hut in the woods off to your right. Take Cable Road for almost a mile.

At the intersection with Nauset Road, take a right and follow it for almost a mile. When you come to the stop light at the intersection with Route 6, take a right.

Follow Route 6 north for 2.7 miles, passing the Wellfleet Drive-In on your left.

At the next stop light, get into the right lane, and keep an eye out for the signs for Marconi. Take a right onto Marconi Beach Road.

Go 500 feet and take a left onto Marconi Station Road. Follow this until the end, and look for the signs saying "Marconi Station" (not to be confused with Marconi Beach, a few miles to the south). Park in the tear drop-shaped parking lot and follow the boardwalk to the overlook.

Description:
Forget the telegraph — in 1901, Guglielmo Marconi set up an experimental station here for transatlantic wireless. It only took a couple years. On January 18, 1903, President Teddy Roosevelt was able to use the station to send a radio message to King Edward VII in Great Britain. Under the canopy by the cliff is a model of the cat's cradle of wires that made up Marconi's site.

Marconi's genius fast outlived the equipment here, and he opened a new facility in Chatham Port, a stone's throw from where William Nickerson first settled in 1664.

Also, as you look down the cliff, try to imagine what it must have been on the night of April 26, 1717, when a nor'easter blew the pirate ship *Whydah* onto the shore, not too far from here.

Wellfleet Historical Society Museum. *Author's photo.*

16) Wellfleet Historical Society Museum

266 Main Street, Wellfleet, MA
508 349-9157
www.wellfleethistoricalsociety.com
• Distance: 5 miles
• Driving Time: 15 minutes

Directions:

Leave the parking lot and follow Marconi Station Road back to Marconi Beach Road. Take a right at the stop sign and proceed to the stop light. Take a right onto Route 6 and follow it for 3.2 miles. You will see a cemetery on your right and a stop light. Get into the left lane. Take a left at the stop light and follow Main Street for one-half mile. The Historical Society is on the right, at 266 Main Street.

Description:

Wellfleet started off as the North Precinct of Eastham, and quickly coalesced around its large harbor on Cape Cod Bay, and its prolific oyster beds. When it became its own town in 1763, the founders chose the name Wellfleet, hoping to confusr the local product with that of eastern England called Wellfleet Oysters. If you ever get a chance to come her for the Oyster Festival in the October, it'll be clear who won that brand recognition contest.

The museum is a good place to ask about the lost village of Billingsgate, and the Great Island tavern. It is said that the tavern was where the pirate Black Bellamy, captain of the *Whydah*, was to rendezvous -- until the deadly wreck on the back shore of the Cape.

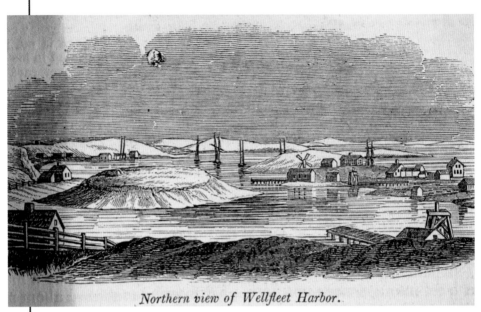

Northern view of Wellfleet Harbor.

Wellfleet Harbor as seen from the north, 1839. *Courtesy of NOAA's America's Coastlines Collection.*

Wellfleet Town Marina. *Author's photo.*

17) Wellfleet Town Marina
255 Commercial Street, Wellfleet, MA
508 349-0320
www.townofwellfleetmarina.com
- Distance: 0.8 miles
- Driving Time: 3 minutes

Directions:
Take a right onto Main Street. Follow this for one block, then take a sharp left onto Bank Street. Go down Bank Street for 500 feet to a stop sign. Take a right onto Commercial Street. Follow Commercial Street for one half mile until your reach the pier. Turn left into the parking lot and park.

Description:
You wouldn't know it now, but the oyster beds of Wellfleet all disappeared in 1770, victim to an unknown plague. Faced with the loss of one resource, the locals turned to others, and it was whaling that really brought cash to Wellfleet.

It wasn't too hard to start, as marine mammals like pilot whales often lose their way in Cape Cod Bay and head due east, driving themselves right into the bay shore of Wellfleet. This was a boon for the Nauset and later colonists alike. These days, we're much more likely to call the National Marine Life Center in Buzzards Bay (see the Canal area Tour).

To end...
We started off at one Cape Cod Bay Harbor and end at another. There's no better place to wrap this up. If you've timed it right, the sun may be setting over Wellfleet Harbor. Nearby are fish markets and restaurants. Wellfleet is a gallery town these days, so investigate it. And if you're up for some more cutting-edge theatre, check out the Wellfleet Harbor Actors Theatre — their offices are next to the pier. Or, if you missed your chance in Rock Harbor, make plans for some fishing — there are charter boats along the pier.

We here overtook two Italian boys, who had waded thus far down the Cape through the sand, with their organs on their backs, and were going on to Provincetown. What a hard lot, we thought, if the Provincetown people should shut their doors against them! Whose yard would they go to next? Yet we concluded that they had chosen wisely to come here, where other music than that of the surf must be rare."
– Henry David Thoreau, *Cape Cod*

Provincetown. Courtesy of Cape Cod Aerial Photography.

Provincetown from the causeway. *Courtesy of capecardart.com.*

There could be no other town like it. If you were sensitive to crowds, you might expire in summer from human propinquity. On the other hand, if you were unable to endure loneliness, the vessel of your person could fill with dread during the long winter.
— Norman Mailer, *Tough Guys Don't Dance*

Safe Haven and Cultural Petri Dish

Provincetown

Overall Distance: Walking 2.1 miles
Time: 3 hours
Public Restrooms: Provincetown Museum, Town Hall, MacMillan Pier, Public Library

Note: One section is in sand, along the shore. Because of their age, many buildings are not ADA-compliant. If you park at the monument, the return back up the hill is long and steep. Try not to drive here. I can't say that enough. There are other options.
The Flex Bus: 1 hr 50 min from Harwich Port
The Provincetown shuttle (summer):
    15 min from North Truro
800 352-7155
www.thebreeze.info

Best advice: This is a shorter walking tour. My experience has been half the time people go to P-Town for whale watching, and half the time they go for shopping and to hang out. This assessment probably horrifies some Provincetowners. But I'm only talking about day-trippers.

So you're probably going to do one or the other. If you're here to shop, dine, or socialize, then save it until we're done. If you want to go on a whale watch, you can either schedule this tour to be broken up in the middle by one — we're heading down to the pier anyway. Or you can save it until the end.

There are no Puritans in P-Town. Actually, there never were. The Pilgrims were not Puritans, as I learned again and again in high school history. The Puritans wanted to "purify" the Church of England from within, with the Separatists (as the Plymouth Pilgrims were known at the time) wanted to separate from the Church and live their own way.

The Puritans went to Boston and founded their city on a hill in 1630. The Separatists arrived ten years earlier in Plymouth and spread out across the Cape and southeastern Massachusetts. Compared to a highly-ordered urban society, then, we've been the relatively laid-back, rural folk who lived at the end of the road.

So when you're living in a sparsely populated area, you tend to rely upon those around you, even if they're a little different. In typical Yankee fashion, you may think they're crazy as a loon, but you kept that to yourself.

Tolerance borne of desperation, so to speak. It began here, four centuries ago. What you see today is just the latest manifestation.

Pilgrim Monument & Provincetown Museum. *Author's photo.*

1) Pilgrim Monument & Provincetown Museum

1 High Pole Hill Road, Provincetown, MA
508 487-1310
www.pilgrim-monument.org
- Distance: 550 feet
- Time: 4 minutes

Directions:

P-Town is another end-of-the road place. No one's passing through. If you're already staying here, great. If you're coming from out of town, be aware that parking is limited and often expensive — except maybe on a weekday in the winter.

All public transit drops off at Lopes Square, at the head of MacMillan Pier. With your back to the wharf, cross Commercial Street and follow Standish Street one block to Bradford Street. Turn left on Bradford Street, walk 200 feet and cross the street to the driveway for the Provincetown monument.

If you're coming by car, free on-street parking is available far down Commercial Street, coming into town. Approaching on Route 6, you'll see the official state "ENTERING PROVINCETOWN" sign in the median strip. Get into the left lane and look for the next exit – a left turn.

Proceed down Snail Road until it hits Commercial Street. Cape Cod Bay is directly across. Take a right and drive a little more than a tenth of a mile. The road forks here, with Bradford Street veering to the right, and Commercial Street going straight. Continue straight on Commercial Street. It is now a one-way road all the way through town. Try to park at least 0.8 mile up the street. Continue straight into town until you hit Lopes Square. Follow the public transit directions above to the monument.

The other driving alternative is to stay on Route 6 and follow the signs to the Pilgrim Monument. You can park there for a fee. But at the end of the tour, you're going to have a steep walk back up the hill to your car.

If you are coming by bike, you're a genius. Ditch it at the Monument.

Provincetown Harbor from the lawn of the Pilgrim Monument. *Author's photo.*

Bas Relief, Town Green. *Author's photo.*

Description:

I'm not going to attempt to replicate anything the museum does — and they know P-Town. Instead, take the chance to go up to top of the Monument and take a look at it all — the town, the harbor, the Cape. See where you've come and where you'll be headed.

Since nearly 1620, P-Town has been trying to dispel the popular misconception that Plymouth was the first stop of the Pilgrims. No, this was where they came after being unable to navigate south beyond the Chatham bars.

You'll see the green spire of Town Hall below. In 1852, the town hall used to be up here on High Pole Hill, and it was here that the *Cape Cod Pilgrim Memorial Association* first tried to get a monument placed. Failing that, a few years later Chief Justice Lemuel Shaw (whose birthplace is visited in the Route 6A tour) succeeded in having a smaller marble tablet placed before the Town Hall. Lost in a fire in 1877, bits of the tablet were discovered when excavating of the present monument began thirty years later.

2) Town Green

Bradford and Ryder Streets, Provincetown, MA
- Distance: 0.2 mile
- Time: 7 minutes

Directions:

From the museum, take a right and walk down the hill to Bradford Street. Take a right onto Bradford Street and follow for 300 feet. The park is on the right, across from Town Hall.

Description:

So what they did — "they" meaning the Pilgrims — was to take refuge here after that long, cramped and bumpy ride across the Atlantic. The harbor was huge and protected on three sides. They spent five weeks trying to figure out what to do: try again to go south to the Hudson (see Chatham Tour), or find someplace here. P-Town might be okay, but they couldn't find a source of fresh water. And after raiding the Nausets' winter stores of corn in Truro, the Pilgrims weren't really on the best terms with the locals. It was getting colder, and five people had already died.

But before they set foot on land, they pledged to cooperate with each other and submit to laws they passed — even though half the party were not Separatists, but just some people, like Stephen Hopkins (father of Giles), they picked up in London to help pay for the trip over. They all agreed to work together.

That was the Mayflower Compact. Then they elected John Carver as their governor. It was very, very different from any other colonial government set down before, in striking contrast to their English cousins in Virginia, and set a tone for New England that would carry through to this day.

The bas relief of the Mayflower Compact signing was erected for its 300th anniversary in 1920.

Provincetown Town Hall. *Courtesy of capecardart.com.*

Doughboy statue. *Author's photo.*

3) Provincetown Town Hall

260 Commercial Street, Provincetown, MA 02657
508 487-7000
www.provincetown-ma.gov
- Distance: 250 feet
- Time: 1 minute

Directions:

Cross the Bradford Street to right side of Ryder Street. Enter Town Hall on the right side.

Description:

Now all this heady American history may seem to stand in stark relief to all the alternative life-styling that abounds in P-Town. If you believe so, then you're going to have an even harder time with all the monuments and memorials to Provincetowners who served and died for the United States. An explanation lies inside Town Hall.

As you enter, you'll see the various paintings adorning the walls. The only other government building I am aware of that contains so many original masterpieces per square inch — aside from galleries — is the Massachusetts State House.

Charles Hawthorne is to thank. There's something about the light here, and is only found in certain parts of the world, like North Africa. A painter, Hawthorne started the Cape Cod School of Art here in 1899. The previous year, the Portland Gale had dealt a heavy blow to the fishing fleet, around which the town's economy had been booming. This left a surplus of unused waterfront buildings for artists to occupy. Seventeen years later *The Boston Globe* declared P-Town the "Biggest Art Colony in the World." And the tourists came to gawk.

Provincetown street folk. *Author's photo.*

Unitarian
Universalist
Meeting House.
Author's photo.

Whaler's Wharf. *Author's photo.*

Interior of the new
Whaler's Wharf.
Author's photo.

4) Unitarian Universalist Meeting House

236 Commercial Street, Provincetown, MA 02657
www.uumh.org
- Distance: 500 feet
- Time: 1 minute

Directions:

Exiting Town Hall, take a right onto Commercial Street and walk 350 feet. The Meeting House is set back from the sidewalk another 80 feet.

Description:

In 1847, whaling and other fisheries were bringing a lot of cash to a town under constant threat of being overtaken by sand dunes. With that wealth, they built this grand edifice.

The congregation had begun twenty-seven years earlier, when two girls found a book on Universalism floating in the water off Long Point. The message of tolerance and acceptance obviously hit the right tone here, and it swept the community. These days, you're as likely to watch a concert there as to hear a sermon. More likely.

5) Whaler's Wharf

237 Commercial Street, Provincetown, MA 02657
508 487-4269
www.newartcinemas.com
- Distance: 500 feet
- Time: 1 minute

Directions:

Leaving the Meeting House, cross Commercial Street and look for the overhead sign for Whalers Wharf to the right.

Description:

Whalers Wharf was always the most bizarre collection of stores, hosting crafts by local artists, laid out in such a way you really weren't sure which way you had come in and how to get out. In February 1998, while I was off in Southeast Asia looking for the wreck of John Kendrick's *Lady Washington*, a fire broke out and took down the building and two others. 450 firefighters from 39 departments across two counties responded that night, and kept the inferno from engulfing any more in P-Town's closely-packed streets.

Provincetown Theatre monument. *Author's photo.*

Remains of the wharf. *Author's photo.*

6) Provincetown Theatre Marker
Rear of Whaler's Wharf
237 Commercial Street,
Provincetown, MA 02657
• Distance: 250 feet
• Time: 5 minutes

Directions:
Continue straight through Whaler's Wharf toward the opposite end. Exit to the beach and the harbor. The marker is on your right.

Description:
Now, I didn't want to confuse you with the new building you just walked through. The building that burned down had originally been the Provincetown Theatre. Eugene O'Neill was present for the premiere of the film adaptation of his play *Anna Christie* in 1919. Three years earlier, his first play, *Bound East for Cardiff*, premiered at Lewis Wharf, further down Commercial Street. A pier at the foot of Gosnold Street, nearby, hosted the Playhouse-on-the-Wharf, featuring original work by O'Niell, Susan Glaspell, Tennessee Williams, and Edward Albee.

Provincetown Theatre, photographed by Carl Van Vechten.
Courtesy of Library of Congress.

MacMillan Pier. *Author's photo.*

Schooner *Hindu. Author's photo.*

7) MacMillan Pier
Lopes Square, Provincetown, MA 02657
508 487-7030
www.provincetownpublicpiercorporation.com
• Distance: 0.25 mile
• Time: 8 minutes

Directions:
From the theatre marker, turn around and walk along the beach for 500 feet. When you reach the pavement, turn right and walk toward the fish market at the foot of Cabral Pier. When you reach it, DO NOT CONTINUE ALONG THIS PIER. Instead, turn left and walk along the sidewalk for 400 feet, keeping the water on your right and the parking lot on your left. When you come to the road leading down MacMillan Pier, turn right on the sidewalk and continue along toward the whale watch boats.

Description:
Recently renovated completely, MacMillan Pier was dedicated to arctic explorer Donald B. MacMillan. Born here in 1874, he was orphaned at age 12. He explored the arctic under Robert Peary, and on his own expedition to Greenland in 1913, was stranded for four years. During that isolation, he made plans for a vessel that could withstand the polar ice, and in 1921 the schooner Bowdoin was launched. He continued his explorations to the arctic over the next 30 years.

The entire shore of the harbor at one time was covered with wharves. There is still a fishing fleet here, though much diminished by economics, federal regulation, and overfishing. But sailing vessels still visit and call the pier home. If you're not up for whale watching, your might consider a sunset cruise on a schooner for true Provincetown authenticity.

Whale's fluke. *Courtesy of capecardart.com.*

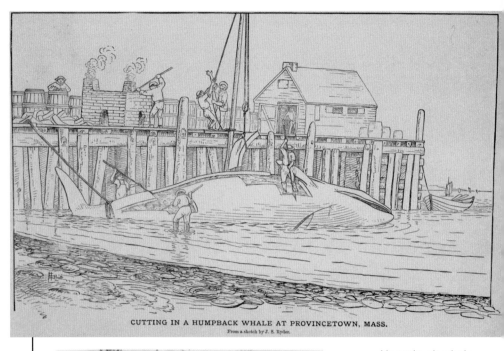

CUTTING IN A HUMPBACK WHALE AT PROVINCETOWN, MASS.

From a sketch by J. S. Ryder.

Humpback whale.
*Courtesy of NOAA's
Historic Fisheries
Collection.*

Arctic explorer Donald
MacMillan aboard the
*Bowdoin. Photoprint
by McDougall & Keefe,
Boothbay Harbor, ME,
courtesy of Library of
Congress.*

Mother and calf. *Courtesy of capecardart.com.*

Provincetown Harbor from Picket & Co. fish wharf, Worth, 1891.
Stefan Claesson, Courtesy of National Archives.

Whydah Pirate Museum. *Author's photo.*

Long Point Light. *Author's photo.*

8) The Whydah Museum

MacMillan Pier, Provincetown, MA 02657
508 487-7030/8899
whydah.com
• Distance: 650 feet
• Time: 5 minutes

Directions:

Walk down the sidewalk of MacMillan Pier for 650 feet. The Museum is prominently on your right.

Description:

If you already took the Outer Cape Tour, you'll recall pirate Black Bellamy and the wreck of the *Whydah* on the back shore of Wellfleet in 1717. Well, here's where his story started, plus that of its discovery by Barry Clifford 25 years ago. The artifacts keep coming up, and other shipwreck explorations take off from here, under the direction of the Center for Historic Shipwreck Preservation.

Not enough sunblock, Whydah Pirate Museum. *Author's photo.*

9) Ferry Terminal & Long Point

MacMillan Pier, Provincetown, MA 02657
• Distance: 350 feet
• Time: 1 minutes

Directions:

Leaving the museum, turn right and continue to the end of the pier. There is a large blue canopy and benches at the ferry dock.

Description:

The best, best way to arrive into Provincetown is by water. Seasonal ferries from Boston and Plymouth dock here at the pier. Even without the voyage, you can still get a decent view of Long Point Light, at the very tip of the Cape, directly ahead.

The first light there was built in 1826, within an already thriving community. It was replaced in 1875. You might notice that, unlike all the other lighthouses we've seen so far, it is square. Don't confuse it with one just up the beach, at Wood End — it was built as an identical replica.

Provincetown Public Library. *Author's photo.*

10) Provincetown Public Library

356 Commercial Street, Provincetown, MA
508 487-7094
www.ptownlib.com
- Distance: 0.4 mile
- Time: 10 minutes

Directions:

From the end of the pier, turn around and follow the right hand sidewalk back to Lopes Square. As you are walking, you can see the white tower of the library off to your right.

Once you are at Commercial Street, take a right. Follow Commercial street for another 600 feet. The Library will be on your left, at the corner with Center Street. Enter through the left side.

Description:

Before you go in, check out the statue, The Tourists, out front. Do not confuse it with other, more lifelike examples nearby.

If it looks more like a church than a library, you're right. It was the Center Methodist Episcopal Church when it was built in 1860 (more whaling money). The church moved in 1955, and a few years later Walter Chrysler opened the Chrysler Art Museum (flush with the proceeds from the recent sale of the Chrysler Building in New York).

That remained for twelve years, and eventually became the Provincetown Heritage Museum, with the half scale model of the *Rose Dorothea* schooner on the second floor. Passing to the Provincetown Library in 2001, it was completed renovated in 2007. Information and photos of the *Rose Dorothea* abound, included her demise in 1917 by a German U-boat.

Half-scale
model of the
Rose Dorothea,
Provincetown
Public Library.
Author's photo.

Provincetown
Art Association
and Museum.
*Photo by
Anton Grassl.
Courtesy of
PAAM.*

Hofmann
Gallery at
Provincetown
Art Association
and Museum.
*Photo by
Anton Grassl.
Courtesy of
PAAM.*

11) Provincetown Art Association & Museum
460 Commercial Street,
Provincetown, MA 02657
508 487-1750
www.paam.org
- Distance: 0.33 mile
- Time: 8 minutes

Directions:
From the front of the Library, turn left on Commercial Street. Follow the sidewalk for several blocks. The museum is on your left, at the corner with Bangs Street.

Description:
We really couldn't finish up Provincetown without coming to one art museum. Although much of his work hangs in Town Hall, PAAM is the museum Charles Hawthorne founded with fellow artists in 1914. Its mission statement is clear and simple: to exhibit and collect art works of merit, and to educate the public in the arts. The modern wing set against the original building is an obvious example of the competing impulses of P-Town of nostalgia and innovation.

12) Provincetown Cemetery
Cemetery Road, Provincetown, MA 02657
- Distance: 0.33 mile
- Time: 8 minutes

Directions:
If you parked your car along Commercial Street, and you're ready to wrap up your day here, you may want retrieve it now. If you parked at the monument or came to town by other means, you might as well continue on foot.

By car, continue down Commercial Street, turn right on Standish Street, and follow it for three blocks to Cemetery Road.

By foot, return down Commercial Street to the library. Take a right on Center Street, and follow it across Bradford Street. When the road turns sharply to the right, take a left off the pavement, and into the parking lot. Cross the parking lot to the cemetery on the other side of the hedge.

Provincetown Cemetery. *Author's photo.*

It's just Beauty that's calling me, the beauty of the far off and unknown, the need of the freedom of great wide spaces, the joy of wandering on and on—in quest of the secret which is hidden over there, beyond the horizon.

— Eugene O'Neill, *Beyond the Horizon*